DEEPER MAGIC
CRAFTING A MEANINGFUL & SPIRITUAL LIFE

— SHARON J BALSAMO —

© 2021 Sharon J Balsamo
All rights reserved. No part of this book may be reproduced in any form without written permission from the author.

Printed in the USA

10 9 8 7 6 5 4 3 2 1

ISBN: 978-1-955346-04-7

Cover & Layout Design: Heather Dakota
www.heatherdakota.com

Wyrd & Wyld Publishing
Spokane, WA

Learn more at
www.thewakingjourney.com

This book is dedicated to my children and all the young folks of the world. May your vision and creativity weave a new world into being, one filled with love, play, connection, and equity. Blessed Be.

TABLE OF CONTENTS

Why This Book 10
How This Book Works 11
    My Personal Orientation 12
    Restoring and Healing the Divine Feminine 13
    The Basics 13
    Boundaries, Ethics, Integrity, and Other Considerations 17
January 19
    Monthly Themes 21
    Affirmations 22
    Daily Invocation 22
    Ground and Connect Meditation 23
    Card Spread 24
    Journal Prompts 25
    Monthly Rituals 27
    Practice: Create an Altar 28
    Practice: Spirit Box 29
    Prepare for the Next Celebration 30
    Monthly Reflections 31
    Heart of a Priestess 33

February 35
    Monthly Themes 37
    Affirmations 38
    Daily Invocation 38
    Cord Cutting and Cleansing Meditation 39
    Card Spread 40
    Journal Prompts 41
    Monthly Rituals 43
    Practice: Triple Rose Self-love Anointing Oil 44
    Practice: Consecrating Your Magical Tools 45
    Celebrate Imbolc 46
    Prepare for the Next Celebration 47
    Monthly Reflections 48
    Divine Vessel 50

March 51
- Monthly Themes 53
- Affirmations 54
- Daily Invocation 54
- Safe Space Meditation 55
- Card Spread 57
- Journal Prompts 58
- Monthly Rituals 60
- Practice: Unbinding Spell 61
- Celebrate the Spring Equinox 62
- Crafting a Wand 63
- Monthly Reflections 66
- Home 68

April 70
- Monthly Themes 72
- Affirmations 73
- Daily Invocation 73
- Worshipping the Maiden Meditation 74
- Card Spread 75
- Journal Prompts 76
- Monthly Rituals 78
- Practice: Honoring the Maiden through Self-worship 79
- Practice: Vision Board 80
- Prepare for the Next Celebration 81
- Monthly Reflections 82
- Ode to my Body 84

May 85
- Monthly Themes 87
- Affirmations 88
- Daily Invocation 88
- Inner Teacher Meditation 89
- Card Spread 91
- Journal Prompts 92
- Monthly Rituals 94
- Practice: Sigils 95
- Celebrate Walpurgisnacht/Beltane 96

- Prepare for the Next Celebration 98
- Monthly Reflections 99
- Carrying the Bones 101

June 103
- Monthly Themes 105
- Affirmations 106
- Daily Invocation 106
- Expansion Meditation 107
- Card Spread 108
- Journal Prompts 109
- Monthly Rituals 111
- Practice: Developing Intuition 112
- Practice: Sex Magic and Queen Talisman 113
- Celebrate Summer Solstice 114
- Monthly Reflections 117
- Queen 119

July 120
- Monthly Themes 122
- Affirmations 123
- Daily Invocation 123
- Energy Hygiene and Protection Meditation 124
- Card Spread 125
- Journal Prompts 126
- Monthly Ritual 128
- Practice: Black Protection Salt 129
- Practice: Protection Herb Bundles 130
- Prepare for the Next Celebration 130
- Monthly Reflections 131
- Self-love is a Boundary 133

August 134
- Monthly Themes 136
- Affirmations 137
- Daily Invocation 137
- Snake Meditation 138
- Card Spread 139
- Journal Prompts 140

Monthly Rituals 142
　　Practice: Creativity Spell Bag 143
　　Practice: Create an Inspiring Playlist 144
　　Celebrate Lughnasa 146
　　Prepare for the Next Celebration 147
　　Monthly Reflections 148
　　The Timing is Now 150

September 151
　　Monthly Themes 153
　　Affirmations 154
　　Daily Invocation 154
　　Tending the Womb-space Meditation 155
　　Card Spread 156
　　Journal Prompts 157
　　Monthly Rituals 159
　　Practice: Daily Gratitude 160
　　Practice: Create a Pentacle 160
　　Celebrate Autumn Equinox 162
　　Prepare for the Next Celebration 164
　　Monthly Reflections 165
　　Mother 167

October 168
　　Monthly Themes 170
　　Affirmations 171
　　Daily Invocation 171
　　Inner Wise Woman Meditation 172
　　Card Spread 174
　　Journal Prompts 175
　　Monthly Rituals 177
　　Practice: Personal Power Potion and Shadow Integration 178
　　Practice: Scrying 179
　　Celebrate Samhain 180
　　Monthly Reflections 181
　　Shadow Monster 183

November 185
    Monthly Themes 187
    Affirmations 188
    Daily Invocation 188
    Welcoming the Ancestors Meditation 189
    Card Spread 190
    Journal Prompts 191
    Monthly Rituals 193
    Practice: Create an Ancestor Altar 194
    Practice: Create a Smoke Blend 195
    Prepare for the Next Celebration 196
    Monthly Reflections 197
    Permission 199

December 200
    Monthly Themes 202
    Affirmations 203
    Daily Invocation 203
    Journey with your Crone Meditation 204
    Card Spread 205
    Journal Prompts 206
    Monthly Rituals 208
    Practice: Dreamwork 209
    Practice: Make a Dream Pouch 209
    Celebrate Winter Solstice 210
    Monthly Reflections 212
    Dream Into Being 214

Now What? 216
Resources 218
Acknowledgments 220
About the Author 221
More for your Waking Journey 222

DEEPER MAGIC

CRAFTING A MEANINGFUL & SPIRITUAL LIFE

SHARON J BALSAMO

WHY THIS BOOK

THANK YOU so much for choosing this book. It is a true labor of my deep love for my spiritual path, for my clients, and for the world as it is awakening and unfolding into a more loving, sustainable, and equitable way of being. I have chosen the title "Deeper Magic" to address our yearning to connect more deeply with a personally spiritual path. This book is for anyone who says: "I want a meaningful and magical spiritual practice, but I don't know where to start!" OR "I have a spiritual practice but I'm struggling to feel deeply connected to the Divine in my daily life." As spirituality and healing are increasingly commodified, with gurus everywhere telling us how to think, feel, and behave, claiming they have the "right" path to follow, I see a common tendency for spiritual seekers to give their personal power and authority away because they don't trust their inner wisdom enough to find a way toward deeper self-awareness and personal awakening.

We live in a time of returning home to ourselves and the deep magic we have within us. It is evident that putting our faith and personal power in the hands of others no longer serves the collective. Our systems are failing us. It is time to tune into our profound inner wisdom that lives in our bodies, hearts, blood, and ancestral memories. In a world that programs us to doubt, fear, and hate ourselves, learning to trust ourselves and our unique connections with Spirit and the Earth becomes ever more important. In this way, we are able to dream and create the world we want to live in. This book will help you remember who you came here to be, what you desire most, and how to call those hopes into existence.

You are magical just as you are. You are connected to the wisdom of the Earth, Spirit, and your ancestors. You have all you need to be guided on your personal path and access your deeper magic. This book will help you learn more about yourself, trust yourself, and find a path that is right for you. Your personal spiritual path is the way to access your inner brilliance (no guru or certification or workshop can ever do that for you). Your unique brilliance is what this world needs most right now.

HOW THIS BOOK WORKS

THIS BOOK supports your personal growth journey and deepens your magic. It is not meant to be a substitute for therapy, or an end-all, be-all philosophy, or the only practice for your life. It will not teach you "how to be a witch" or make you a "guru" to facilitate healing for others. Hopefully, it will open doorways and illuminate new paths for you to explore as you navigate the path that is in greatest alignment for *you*. It is meant to help you learn more about yourself, your programming, your wounding, your stories, your beliefs, your practices, and your relationship to the world around you. This leads to a more intentional and fulfilled life.

In the absolute simplest terms, this book works with language and behavior to activate new neuropathways in your conscious mind. In turn, your conscious mind "programs" your subconscious mind, which is what "creates" the world as you perceive it. The practices, magic, rituals, and ceremonies strengthen and reactivate those new neuropathways to reinforce a more loving, empowered way of being in the world. Magic and co-creating with the Divine is complex. It takes time to understand your magic. I highly encourage you to follow your interests, refer to the Resources on Page 218 to learn more.

The universe within you is as real as the universe beyond you. The universe within is made up of your thoughts, feelings, beliefs, neuropathways, behavioral patterns, memories, experiences, traumas, language, stories, bodily sensations, and spiritual experiences. These are what create your perception of the external reality you experience. Having deep awareness and understanding of the universe inside you and how it operates, allows you to have greater power and control over how you create and experience your life in the world around you. This is what is meant by the saying "As within, so without."

Our concept of time is changing—from a linear orientation back to a cyclical one. Cyclical is how our bodies resonate with the Earth and cycles of the seasons. It is important to find your own rhythm of personal growth, as your soul's work continues to evolve throughout your life. Do the practices in this book year-after-year, adapting them as you grow, and deepen your relationship with you inner self and your spiritual journey.

You are welcome to adapt and alter each offering as you see fit. The design is flexible to your unique story and lifestyle. The practices in this book are foundational, universal to many different traditions and lineages and rooted in my lineages of Celtic, Germanic, European, and Christian traditions. Shape the practices to fit your own belief system and lineage.

Anything can be substituted for what is native for the area in which you live and rooted in the traditions you identify with. I encourage you to learn about the plants, ecosystems, and history of the land beneath your feet, where your ancestors originated, and apply your knowledge to your personal magical practice—making your magic personal and more potent.

My Personal Orientations

Of course, this book is deeply influenced by my journey, life experiences, education, and belief system. Here is an abbreviated list of the orientations and education that serve as the foundations of this book:

- Intersectional Feminism *and everything that goes along with it: anti-capitalism, anti-racism, anti-ableism, anti-heterosexism, and more.*
- Existentialism, Gestalt and Jungian psychology, Transpersonal Psychology, Attachment Theory, and Choice Theory
- 12-step programs
- BS in International Studies *the intersection of Political Science, Religious Studies and Anthropology*
- MS Clinical Mental Health Counseling and a practicing Licensed Professional Counselor
- Trainings in: Psychodrama, Brainspotting, Huna, Dialectical Behavioral Therapy, Interpersonal Neurobiology, and Holotropic Breathwork
- My own personal healing journey through EMDR (Eye Movement Desensitization and Reprocessing), group and individual therapy, Shamanic healing, magic and witchcraft, pilgrimages to sacred lands, and narrative and dream work
- Tarot, astrology, witchcraft, animism, and mythology
- My personal religious/spiritual upbringing in the Catholic church, Baha'i Faith, and New Thought ideology

A note on Unverified Personal Gnosis:

When it comes to spiritual principles, beliefs, and practices, as an existentialist, there is no way to know with absolute certainty what is true or untrue. The concept of *Unverified Personal Gnosis* (UPG) allows people to explore what beliefs and practices work best for them. The associations, beliefs, and practices in this book come from my *Personal Gnosis*, some of which is unverified (coming from my personal experiences and associations), some of which is shared (coming from universal concepts). It is up to you to decide what resonates for you on your spiritual path.

Restoring and Healing the Divine Feminine

I was raised in the religions of Catholicism and Baha'i (with a strong influence of Southern Baptist). While growing up, my experiences of the Divine were always male-oriented. As I embarked on my personal spiritual journey as a young woman, I longed to see the Divine reflected in me and my experiences. I yearned to see the feminine as something to be cherished, honored, and worshipped instead of being put second to the masculine. In my practice, I found that many of my clients desired something similar. Therefore, this spiritual lens facilitates the rising of the Divine Feminine to restore balance to a dynamic that is ruled by the manipulation of the Divine Masculine. All of us have healing to do around this imbalance.

This book is meant to be inclusive of everyone who identifies as woman, femme, non-binary, and anyone who feels a connection to the Divine feminine energy within themselves. Use these practices regardless of your gender identity or the gender of your concept of Spirit/Higher Power/God. Spirit and the Divine are used interchangeably in reference to this concept. It uses gender neutral and feminine descriptors and pronouns. Please use the term that resonates with you and your spiritual beliefs.

The Basics

Here are some basic concepts and tools that are used throughout the book:

Archetypes: These are universal characters that we can evoke and embody when we want to call on a certain way of being or energy. You can shape your personal archetypes however you see fit. The practices in this book are designed to cultivate a powerful and personal connection with each archetype within you. When you need an archetypal energy, work with it as a source of inner strength, inspiration, and guidance.

Intention: Creating sacred space and doing spiritual practices is not a complex process; the most basic ingredients are your intention and focus. Anything you do with intention can be sacred and magical. Be clear with yourself about your intentions or focus in spiritual work to achieve profound results.

Affirmations: These use the power of language to directly program your subconscious mind. Each month has specific affirmations for each theme/archetype. Here are some suggestions for working with affirmations:

- Write them on index cards and put them up around your house where you will see them regularly. Or keep them next to your bed and read them to yourself every morning.
- The morning time, right as you are rousing awake, is the most potent time to use affirmations, as your subconscious mind is most open to suggestion. Therefore, don't look at your phone first thing in the morning to read the news, check your email, or scroll through social media! It programs your

subconscious mind with all kinds of garbage. Instead, upon waking, breathe deeply into your body, ground your energy, set your intention for the day, and speak your affirmations. This will set the tone for your day and completely change how you experience your life!

- You can write your own affirmations if the ones here don't quite work for you. Tips to creating potent affirmations:
    - Write them in positive language (do not include no, not, can't, aren't, don't) and in the present tense, as if it is already happening.
    - Make them believable but stretch outside your comfort zone.
    - When you speak the affirmation to yourself, there may be a feeling of lightness, expansiveness, relief, or excitement in your body. If you feel resistance or doubt, choose something else.
    - If you have a negative belief about yourself, write an affirmation that will be the positive counter to that negative belief (for example: if my belief is "life is so exhausting," my affirmation can be "I am energized").

Invocations: These are like prayers that speak your intentions to Spirit and your subconscious. They work similarly to affirmations but allow us to make requests from Spirit and align with unique intentions for each day.

Meditations: This is a discipline that if you can commit to doing consistently, will completely change your life. It is the ultimate learning tool for understanding how your mind operates. Practicing meditation gains mastery over your consciousness, so it works for you and not the other way around. Each meditation in this book is designed to evoke a sensory experience that will program your neuropathways. You can change the imagery and language as it suits you. Recordings of the meditations are available for download so you can listen to them as part of a daily practice. You can also record them in your own voice. Go to the recordings at: www.thewakingjourney.com.

Tarot and Oracle Cards: Whether you are new to a magical practice using cards for divination or you've been doing it for years, the simple spreads in this book will assist you in gaining clarity around your own journey and developing a relationship with your cards. It does not matter what kind of deck you use. Choose one that speaks to you and feels aligned with your energy.

Journaling: This is one of the most potent ways to process our emotions and experiences and build awareness of our inner world, while getting clarity on our desires and intentions.

Plant, Animal, and Stone Magic: Each month has suggested allies from the natural world to work with for the month. The most basic way to work with them is to meditate with their energy and cultivate a working relationship with each ally. This helps you better understand which medicines are most potent for you in your magic and what energies they hold to align with your intentions for your personal practices. If you are drawn to work with different plants, animals, and stones than the ones suggested, honor that and be open to what they wish to teach you, and how they want to work with you. I have deliberately chosen plant allies that are considered "common;" they are easy to find in most grocery stores, herb gardens, and herbal shops, and can easily be substituted for what's native in your area. Similarly, the stones are common, relatively inexpensive, and easy to find from ethical sources.

Suggestions to work with plant magic:
- *Create a ritual salt:* blend with sea salt and other herbs that call to you to use in your magic, like casting a protective circle for spell work, holding a specific intention, or to add to your bath for a ritual cleansing.
- *Make Incense:* grind dry herbs with a mortar and pestle or coffee grinder and burn them on a hot charcoal disk to infuse the air with the medicine of the plant.
- *Make a tea, infusion, or tincture:* soak in boiling water 10 to 15 minutes for tea or overnight for an infusion, or soak in vodka or other high-proof alcohol for 4 to 6 weeks to extract the medicine of the plant. Take a dropperful to ingest the plant's magic.

Suggestions to work with animal magic:
- Meditate with the spirit of the animal, opening yourself up to what they wish to show and teach you.
- Imagine embodying the spirit of that animal; how does it feel? How does the animal behave? How does the animal interact with other beings?
- Journal about what different animals represent to you. For example: how do you feel when you see a crow? What are the main traits of a bear that resonate for you? What does a butterfly communicate to you? Begin to record your symbolism for the animal world to better understand the personal messages they bring you.

Suggestions to work with stone magic:
- Add to potions and spells to amplify the energy of your intentions.
- Carry them in your pockets or spell pouches to keep the energy of the stone close to you.
- Put it under your pillow while sleeping to allow it to work its magic through your dreams.

Ritual Teas: Each month has a recommended ritual tea to embody the spirit of the plant ally and support your personal growth throughout the month. To make a ritual tea, gather your ingredients with intention and blend them, speaking the month's affirmations and/or invocation into the mixture. The general ratio is 1 tsp. of dried tea mixture to 1 cup of hot water. The recipes are formatted so you can make a large or small batch. Water has memory, so the more you speak and direct your energy toward it as you make the tea, the more potent your magic will be. The ritual tea recipes were created by Amanda Swan at the Awakened Table. Learn more about her at https://www.theawakenedtable.com/

Full Moon Ritual Bath: The Full Moon is a time for reflection, releasing magic, or honoring the culmination of a cycle. If you choose to make the moon part of your practice, there are lovely resources on Moon Magic on the internet and in books! See the Resources on Page 218. The monthly Full Moon ritual bath helps you love yourself, deepen your magic, and connect with the energy of the Moon. If you do not have a bathtub or just prefer showers, you can do a foot bath or create a salt scrub with the ingredients by adding sea salt and a carrier oil, such as almond oil, to scrub yourself in the shower, and then rinse. This makes a beautiful Release and Forgiveness Practice during the Full Moon.

New Moon Candle Spells: The time of the New Moon is one of possibilities, a time of darkness, going inward, and connecting with what we are ready to create. During the New Moon, candle spells bring illumination to our desires and plant the seeds of our intentions in the spirit world. As the moon waxes, the seeds will grow to manifest into the physical world. Use white candles for any color candle. Tea light candles work just fine.

Practices: Each practice, spell, and ritual created here is designed to support your journey and deepen your self-awareness, self-love, and your connection to your unique magic. I invite and encourage you to adapt them in ways that feel aligned for you. Make them your own! Also, each spell and practice can be used at any time of year, whenever it feels useful, and adapted for other purposes.

Holidays and celebrations: These are ways to celebrate the passing of the year, the changing of the seasons, and harness the unique magical energy of each time of year. There are suggestions for simple rituals and ways to celebrate these occasions. For the Equinoxes and Solstices, I have chosen to include magic that embodies the element of each season (Winter—Earth; Spring—Air; Summer—Fire; Autumn—Water) to help you deepen your understanding of each element and how to work with them, as well as create basic magical tools you can add to your magical practice if you don't already have them. I welcome you to do your own research on these holidays and create rituals that feel potent and aligned for you. Goddesses to honor for each celebration are suggested, with offerings and invitations to learn more about them. These are deities from my own personal practice that are helpful to connect with. Research your lineages to see what deities call to you. Learn more and honor them on your spiritual journey. *Resources are listed at the end of this book.*

Boundaries, Ethics, Integrity, and other Considerations

As a cisgender white woman on a spiritual path, I have encountered attitudes, beliefs, and practices that have (unknowingly) caused harm to others. Appropriation, commodification, and the burden and deception of white supremacist values on ancient spiritual practices are common. My personal work finds a spiritual path that does not perpetuate these harms and that work will never end. These are lessons I have learned so far and want to share with you: craft a spiritual practice that is not appropriative, exploitative, or harmful to others. If you have not already, I strongly encourage you to embark on your own journey of exploration around the issues of appropriation and commodification, and connect with your powerful lineages as a gateway to your personal magic.

Appropriation: This book focuses on simple magical and spiritual concepts that are universal in many traditions and open to all. Start here. Start with your intuition—what herb wants to be worked with for your spell or ceremony? What feels natural to you in creating a release ritual? Part of the journey is learning to trust yourself, while always staying open to learning and remaining humble. If you already have an established spiritual/magical practice, the practices in this book are designed to be adapted and shaped to work for you.

Educate yourself on closed versus open practices, and be respectful of the practices that are closed to you. A closed practice requires a connection to a specific lineage and/or an initiation of some kind to use it with authority and integrity. If a certain practice intrigues you, take time to research it to better understand where it comes from and whether it is appropriate and accessible for you to practice. Explore your personal lineages, cultures, and the spiritual practices connected to them. Every culture has a universal connection to the cosmos, spirituality, and magic—find yours!

Work with the personal guides, angels, deities, and benevolent ancestors that you know. Cultivate relationships with these spirits through prayers, offerings, and meditations before asking them to help you in your magic. Do not call on deities and spirits that you do not know and have no relationship with.

Protect and cleanse your energy! (In-depth instructions are detailed later in this book.) Learn to discern when you are holding onto and accepting responsibility for energy that is not yours, and when you are projecting your energy onto others. These are boundary violations.

Do not violate the free will of others or do magic to manipulate or control others. For example, doing magic to change someone's personality or desires is a violation of their free will. Instead, do protection magic for yourself, or a spell for justice, balance, or harmony in your relationship with that person. Always seek to do no harm in your magic and spiritual practices. Our intentions are a reflection of our inner state. If we wish to cause harm to another, it is an invitation to look at where we feel harmed and what we need to heal. There are varying philosophies on this. I do not claim that my perspective is the ultimate truth on free will or how you should or shouldn't work with your magic. From my experiences, magic always comes back around. What type of energy do you want to put into the world?

Create clear boundaries around whom you entrust to do this vulnerable and powerful work with you.

Be Responsible. I cannot stress this enough. Be responsible to yourself and consider how you impact others. Be mindful and thoughtful about what you are doing. If you unwittingly do harm, be accountable. Stay humble when you do not know something, or when something is outside your scope of practice. Accept full responsibility for your own thoughts, feelings, beliefs, and behaviors.

Always use sustainable options that are not appropriative! Know where your herbs, crystals, and other tools come from and choose sustainable options. Understand that the sources you use to procure these tools have a great impact and choose local sources whenever possible. Support the businesses of folks of color, queer folks, disabled folks, and other marginalized folks. Use your practice to pay reparations to these folks by patronizing their businesses and promoting their work.

The wellness and spiritual growth industries often prey upon people's insecurities and feelings of unworthiness and profit off them. They benefit from you believing that you will never be good enough and must always seek healing/betterment/perfection. The work in this book is based on the belief that only *you* know where healing and growth are needed. You are perfect, wonderful, and amazing just the way you are. There is no need present an image of perfect transcendence to others. You are human. You are allowed to be flawed, have complex emotions, and stand up for yourself if needed. You are also allowed to be powerful, brilliant, and unconditionally loved. All these ways of being can be true of you simultaneously. I encourage you to notice when you put folks on a pedestal of perfection and seek/expect the same of yourself, as this is a toxic complicity in a white supremacist/capitalist/colonialist lie that such a thing is possible, attainable, and desirable. You do not need the "right tools" to do magic. You only need the magic you hold within. If you don't have material that is mentioned, make do with what you have. Your intention is powerful enough.

This book will not qualify or certify you to call yourself a witch, priestess, shaman, teacher, or facilitator of others' healing! It is for your personal practice only.

Chapter One
JANUARY

"I am a Priestess. I honor the Earth."

JANUARY BEGINS the calendar year and is a time to deepen and re-establish your relationship with the Divine. This month, we explore your relationship with Spirit in your daily life.

Ground ♦ Connect ♦ Trust ♦ Surrender

THE PRIESTESS:

The Priestess archetype is deeply connected to her Divine nature and the spirit realms. She serves the Goddess as a spiritual embodiment of Mother Earth. The Priestess communicates with her guides and nature spirits and walks with one foot in the physical world and one foot in the spiritual realms. She understands the infinite nature of the universe and the limitations of her human mind. The Priestess is comfortable in the mystery, lives in trust and faith, and is of service to her community and planet.

THE WOUND: Separation from the Divine

THE HEALING: Unity/connection with the Divine

ELEMENT: Earth

PLANT ALLY: Juniper
Ancient and highly protective, Juniper is a gateway between the Earthly and Spiritual realms.

ANIMAL ALLY: American Bison
Commonly associated with the unification of Earth and Spirit, the Bison is a symbol of abundance and nurturing, reassuring us that the Divine is within, supporting us when we need it, and reminding us of our Earthly and Divine natures. It is both grounding and deeply magical.

STONE ALLY: Clear Quartz
This stone is the ultimate "starter crystal," used to enhance any intention or spell work we do. It is generally associated with clarity of vision, thought, and intent. Try it to call on the clarity and understanding of the Divine, who sees and understands things that we cannot.

Monthly Themes

Grounding: A practice of reconnecting to an ancient truth. Our body is the conduit of our spiritual experience and connects us to the Earth. The physical body is a source of wisdom and healing, rooting us to our original life source (Mother Earth), providing a way to tap into the loving support of the Creator of your understanding. The Earth offers us stability and an unlimited source of power. Grounding means sending your energy into the Earth through visualization and breath, feeling your roots connecting to the Earth and receiving the nurturing, loving energy from the Earth. This practice is detailed in the monthly meditation.

Connection: Here is where we actively seek a relationship with the Divine, make offerings to show our gratitude, and live in reciprocity with the world around us. We quiet ourselves to receive messages and ask the Divine for what we need. We are never alone. The Divine lives within us, within the Earth, and is accessible in everything at every moment.

Trust: In cultivating a loving relationship with the Divine, we build trust of support that our paths are guided, and we have what we need in each given moment. This allows us to take big leaps of faith in our desires and manifest amazing things.

Surrender: This is the final step, the release that makes it possible for Spirit to take the reins and bring our desires into the physical realm. The idea of surrendering can be frightening and off-putting for some folks. If you notice this coming up for you, sit with the discomfort. Ask yourself what feels scary about the idea of surrender? Often, it is because we do not trust what we are surrendering to. We fear that surrendering will hurt us, take advantage of us, or neglect our tender hearts. Surrender means to let go of the illusion of control. This requires us to trust that someone or something is in control. We must have a solid concept of our own personal Higher Power to foster the trust it takes to surrender fully. When we have faith, we experience more flow, synchronicity, and miracles as Spirit does for us what we cannot do for ourselves.

Grounding, connecting, and trusting in Spirit gives us the foundation to surrender fully, to take the leap into the unknown!

Affirmations

I am an embodiment of the Divine on Earth.

I am loved, supported, and guided by Spirit.

I root deeply into the Earth.

I surrender to my highest path.

My personal affirmations:

_____
_____
_____
_____

Daily Invocation

Spirit, I come to you humbly and with gratitude. I ask that you walk with me today. Please guide me. Show me the miracles at work in my life. Open me to what is possible. Help me trust. Help me surrender fully to my highest path, knowing you are with me every step of the way. Open me to receive your wisdom. Blessed Be.

My personal intentions and prayers:

_____
_____
_____
_____
_____
_____
_____
_____

Ground and Connect Meditation

Begin by centering on your breath. Allow all distracting thoughts to float through your mind and return focus to the breath. Ground into your body and feel your muscles relaxing. Now, imagine a root extending from your tailbone into the Earth, past the floor, into the soil and rock, down past crystals and aquifers, through the magma and rooting into the very core of the Earth. Imagine this cord as hollow. It allows you to tap into the supportive energy of the Earth: nurturing, unconditionally loving, grounding, powerful, and abundant. Feel this energy traveling up the cord and entering your body as a beautiful green light. Notice what it's like to feel this beautiful supportive energy fill your body and settle in your heart space. Ask Mother Earth for whatever assistance you need and offer gratitude and love in return. Now, imagine sending any energy in your body that is ready to be released: worry, heaviness, fear, shame, or guilt. See this energy traveling down the cord and being received by the Earth. See it being transmuted and transformed by the grounding power of the Earth. Offer thanks.

Next, imagine a cord extending from your crown, the very top of your head. See it extending up, past the ceiling, past clouds and moon and sun, out into the stars. Feel it tapping into the energy of the Divine: expansive, wise, all-knowing, inspired, and full of infinite possibility. Call on your guides, angels, and ancestors who are supporting your highest and best expression in this life. See this Divine support coming into your crown as a sparkling golden light. Notice what it's like to feel the golden light filling your body, mixing with the green light from the Earth, in a beautiful swirl of golden-green sparkly light, centering in your heart space. Ask your guides and helpers for whatever support you need. As your heart beats, feel the energy moving through you, expanding, and extending out to your energetic field, and out again into the world. Feel yourself fully immersed in the frequency of unconditional love and gratitude. Send it out into the world. Offer thanks.

Reflections on this meditation:

_____
_____
_____
_____
_____
_____
_____
_____
_____
_____

Card Spread

-1-
What support from Spirit am I receiving right now on my path?

-2-
What support am I resisting? Can I challenge myself to open more to receive?

-3-
What is Spirit asking of me?

-4-
What do I need to surrender to be more aligned with my highest path?

Journal Prompts:

Choose one or more of these questions each week to reflect and explore here or in your journal.

Create a detailed, personal concept/image of the Divine that feels personally safe, loving, and supportive. What qualities do they need for you to trust and allow Them to be in control? Some examples: unconditionally loving, wise, accepting, or gentle. Write, draw or collage your ideas.

What do I need most from the Divine right now in my life? How would it look in my day-to-day?

What kind of relationship do I want with the Divine?

Do I trust the Divine? Why or why not? What do I need from the Divine to be able to trust deeply and surrender completely?

What is my relationship to the Divine right now?

What was I raised to believe about my spirituality?

What comes up for me when I think about God?

What messages did I internalize as a child about God and the Divine?

What feelings, thoughts, and bodily sensations do I experience when I reflect on surrender?

What areas of my life do I feel most powerless over? What feels scary/hard/out of control?

What do I feel ready to surrender in my life right now?

Monthly Rituals

Ritual Tea
- 1 part rooibos tea
- ½ part juniper berries
- ½ part dried ginger (1 part if using fresh ginger)

Crush juniper berries in mortar and pestle. Combine with ginger and rooibos in a small pot of water. Simmer for 15 minutes. Turn off heat. Optional: Add milk and honey to taste. Strain into mug.

Full Moon Ritual Salt Bath
Add ground dried juniper berries and needles to pure sea salt with a few drops of frankincense oil (substitute cedarwood or myrrh oil). Put a few tablespoons into a warm bath with the intention of grounding your energy and connecting with Spirit. Add one cup of Epsom salt for a relaxing effect.

New Moon Candle Spell
Anoint a white candle with frankincense, juniper or cedar essential oil and either sprinkle on or roll in dried juniper needles. Ask for protection, vision, and clarity in communicating with the Divine. Call on your guides to support and protect you throughout the year. Let the candle burn down all the way.

Make sure the candle is in a fire and heat proof container. Do not leave burning candles unattended.

Note: Cedar can be substituted for juniper in the salt bath and candle spell. ***Do not use cedar in tea! It is considered toxic to ingest.***

Practice: How to Create an Altar

Altars are a sacred space in our home where we honor our spiritual work. It grounds and holds energy; essentially it is a portal to the spiritual realms that we create and cultivate. A dresser top, mantel, or windowsill work perfectly. You don't need anything special on an altar. Choose items that carry personal meaning for you. Here are some suggestions:

- an image that evokes the energy of the Divine for you (this could be an animal helper, a depiction of nature, an angel, goddess, or saint—whatever resonates deeply for you. You can also make a collage/vision board of how you envision your Higher Power)
- a clear quartz crystal or bowl of salt (representing the element of Earth)
- incense or herbs for burning (representing Air for smoke)
- a white candle (Representing fire)
- a bowl or chalice with a little water (representing the element of Water)
- altar cloth—a scarf or handkerchief works well

Incorporate the different elements—Earth, Air, Fire, and Water. This brings balance and power to our magic. But again, there are no rules. Connect deeply and intuitively with the objects you are using. Visit your altar daily, connect with Spirit, ground into the Earth, pull a card, and ask for whatever support or assistance you need that day. Make offerings to Spirit of salt, honey, flowers, or anything you like, as a gesture of gratitude for its support and to cultivate a reciprocal relationship to the Divine. Clean, refresh, and change your altar often—monthly, seasonally, or whenever you are called.

My sacred altar objects:

_____
_____
_____
_____
_____
_____
_____
_____
_____
_____
_____

Practice: Surrendering & Spirit Box

This is inspired by 12-step work and is a powerful tool when we feel out-of-control, overwhelmed, anxious, and lacking a feeling of trust and flow in our lives.

1. Write out all the things that feel overwhelming, frustrating, scary, out-of-control, or vexing.
2. Divide them into two categories: What is in my control/What is outside of my control
   If you have a hard time with this, here are some guidelines:

What you have control over:
- your feelings, thoughts, beliefs, attitudes
- how you show up in the world
- how you treat yourself and others
- your actions and behaviors
- your boundaries

What you don't have control over:
- other people's feelings, thoughts, beliefs, attitudes
- how they show up in the world
- how they treat you and others
- their actions and behaviors
- their boundaries
- You do not have control over that which is unknown, what happened in the past, how the future will unfold.

3. For your "What's in my control" list, write one small action plan for each item.
4. For your "What's outside of my control" list, put the list in your "Spirit Box." The list can be burned, thrown away, or buried, too.

Make a "Spirit Box"

You can keep the Spirit Box on your altar to remind you to let go and surrender the things that are outside your control. Spirit will take care of them.

Get a small cardboard box and decorate the outside. Your local craft store has pretty boxes or use a tissue box. Get creative. Don't over think it. Cut a hole in the top of the box, but have it otherwise sealed. Whenever there is something in your life that needs assistance from Spirit, write it down and put it in your Spirit Box. Make a ritual of burning the box at Winter Solstice with your Yule log and make a new Spirit Box for the following year.

Prepare for the Next Celebration!

Imbolc or St. Brigid's Day happens on the 1st or 2nd of February in the Northern Hemisphere and August 1st or 2nd in the Southern Hemisphere. We celebrate this holiday by cleansing and protecting our homes.

You may want to have on-hand:
- White candles
- Incense or herbs to burn
- Water and salt
- Statue or photo of the Goddess Brigid
- Items representing fertility and creativity
- Homemade bread
- Items that represent the energy of spring
- A bell

Gather the items that resonate with you and are easily accessible. There is no need to purchase anything new, unless you really want to! Suggestions for celebrating Imbolc are detailed in February (see Page 46).

Monthly Reflections

What was most challenging for me this month?
_____
_____
_____

What was most rewarding? What growth have I witnessed in myself?
_____
_____
_____

Magical associations to the Priestess/Divine:
_____
_____
_____

Tree, herb, flower, and plant allies I worked with:
_____
_____
_____

Animal allies I worked with:
_____
_____
_____

Stone allies I worked with:

Songs:

Scents:

Food and drink:

People, Deities, and Role Models:

My Personal Practices: *What am I learning about my personal magic through these practices?*

Heart of a Priestess

I am a priestess.

A priestess of this land, of the cedar tree, of the waterfall.
I give offerings of heart-shaped stones.

My heart.

I am stone. I carry the wisdom of generations.
Of centuries.
I carry memories of tumbling rivers and
lava flows and moss growing slowly,
quietly.

I come to the water for healing.
The wind lifts me
Up, up, up
to see the grander view.
I hover over treetops.

I am an eagle.
My vision is clear.
My wings are freedom.
My voice is truth.

There is joy here under this rushing waterfall.
There is a remembering of love,
of gratitude,
of connecting with my sisters.

My sister priestesses.

I love them, and they love me.

Our temple is my body,
the embodiment of Earth magic—
curves and twists and juicy flowing delicious gorgeousness
of smooth skin
hard bone
WILD HAIR and
shining eyes and
truth and divinity and
sacred dark places
where mystery lives.

Where magic lives.

Our temple is the waterfall
the cedar trees
the muddy decay in moss and soil and pine cones.

Our temple is the sky
the volcano
the rose.

It is all holy.
It is all the Goddess.
It is all possibility and
loving and
grieving and
HOWLING and
singing a song, you didn't know was in you.

My sacred gift is to speak,
to write,
to honor the temple of the Goddess.
To live a truth that has long been forgotten.

The heart remembers.

Chapter Two
FEBRUARY

"I am a healer, I tend to my wounds."

WELCOME TO FEBRUARY. We begin the month celebrating Imbolc, the gateway to spring. When winter begins thawing into the growing season, it is a time of deep healing and cleansing as preparation to sow the seeds of intention.

Heal ◆ Release ◆ Forgive ◆ Cleanse

The Healer

The Healer archetype has deep awareness of their woundings and traumas and holds this wounding with great care and reverence. They understand their own responsibility for healing and do not cling to victimhood or helplessness. The Healer shows up for others in their wounding, holding profound space to witness the pain and suffering of the world within and without. This archetype understands that the path to healing is through unconditional love, patience, and forgiveness.

The Wound: Victimhood/trauma

The Healing: Unconditional love and forgiveness

Element: Earth

Plant Ally: Rose
Rose is a high-vibrational flower that embodies the energy of unconditional love. Soothing to the nervous system, the rose brings a sense of peace, tranquility, and loving support from the Divine.

Animal Ally: Swan
The Swan is a creature of beauty and grace. It is associated with the story of the Ugly Duckling, who experienced deep wounding of abandonment, disconnection, and pain, only to become a beautiful and magnificent creature, despite these wounds. The Swan reminds us that even though we carry wounds, we are becoming exactly who and what we are meant to be, creatures of great beauty and power.

Stone Ally: Rose Quartz
A heart healer and stone of forgiveness and unconditional love, Rose Quartz is the perfect ally for our inner Healer. It soothes emotional wounds and brings softness to our intentions and magic.

Monthly Themes

Heal: We all have wounds. It is the nature of being human and alive on this planet. Trauma happens. The trouble is that we are not taught what it means to heal and instead are encouraged to hide and deny our wounds. This only causes our wounds to fester, which turns into resentment, bitterness, and powerlessness. We become stuck in a story of our own victimhood. Then the wounding only perpetuates, as we project our wounding onto other people, unable to take responsibility for our healing.

This month you're invited to be in loving relationship with your wounds, so you can heal. When we heal ourselves, we have the capacity to hold loving space for others to heal.

Emotional, mental, and spiritual wounds are exactly like physical wounds in that they will heal naturally given the right conditions. Maybe they need outside support, but with that support and a nurturing environment, healing will happen. We do not have to do our healing alone, but we alone are responsible for our healing.

The healing process is cyclical: we often feel old wounds arise that we thought were healed, only to discover they are asking for healing on another level. Whenever we "up-level" on our journey, we often need to look at and re-integrate these wounds to weave them into a new story of who we are now.

Release: In the cycles of living, we must let go of old, outdated ways of being to create space for new growth. When we learn to release that which doesn't serve us, we level up our spiritual work and manifest the world we want to live in. Releasing is a practice of allowing ourselves to let go.

Forgiveness: Forgiveness is a key to our healing so we can let go of our energetic attachments to what caused our wounding and focus on what we need to move forward and grow. A common 12-step saying is: "Resentment is like drinking poison and waiting for the other person to die." Holding onto resentment toward ourselves and others is toxic to us. Forgiveness is the antidote.

Cleanse: When we've done deep healing, release, and forgiveness work, cleansing ourselves physically and energetically helps shift into the energy we want to embody moving forward. It is part of our energetic hygiene that keeps us open to new growth.

Affirmations:

I forgive myself and others.

I release bitterness.

I am healing and growing.

My wounds are my teachers.

My personal affirmations:

_____

_____

_____

_____

Daily Invocation:

Spirit, today I choose healing. Today I choose forgiveness. Help me find softness with myself, help me have compassion for those who have harmed me. Release me of all bitterness. Show me my wounded places, so I may love them to transform them. Blessed Be.

My personal intentions and prayers:

_____

_____

_____

_____

_____

_____

_____

_____

Cord Cutting and Cleansing Meditation

Take a few deep breaths and close your eyes, ground yourself into Mother Earth, feeling her loving, nurturing energy filling your body with unconditional love. Let this loving energy radiate out of you. Feel it flowing freely and abundantly from the Earth through you.

Imagine someone in your life with whom there is tension, grief, or unresolved business in your relationship. See them standing before you. Look at them with love, sending Mother Earth's unconditional, loving energy. Watch this loving energy envelope the other person completely.

See the energetic cord that connects you to this person. What does it look like? What is the quality of it, and how do you experience it? Where is it on your body? There may be more than one.

Imagine a beautiful silver blade coming down and severing the cord. See the cord dissolve and disappear. Notice what it feels like for the cord to be gone.

Speaking to the other person, say "I release you. I thank you. I love you."

Do this with as many people as you like.

Once complete, imagine clearing the space in your mind with your breath. Close the door on that space and imagine yourself walking outside to a beautiful flowing river. Notice what you feel emotionally and physically after cutting this cord.

Enter the river and allow the water to wash away any residual energy, resentments, or negativity. Feel the water refresh your soul, energize you and light up your cells with pure, clear, healing water. Feel the water running along your skin, in between your toes, in your hair. Give thanks for this sacred cleansing water. When you feel complete, come out of the river, lie down on the soft grass, and feel the sun warm your skin as it dries you. Stay here as long as you like. Know you can return to this space whenever it is needed. When you are ready, return your awareness to your body, your breath, and the present moment. You are complete.

Reflections on this meditation:

_____
_____
_____
_____
_____
_____
_____
_____

Card Spread

-1-
How does my wounding manifest in my life now?

-2-
What is supporting my healing?

-3-
What energetic attachments are ready to be released that no longer serve me?

-4-
What is the medicine (or learning) of my wounds?

Journal Prompts:

Choose one or more of these questions each week to reflect and explore here or in your journal.

What wounds do I still carry from my past? What memories, experiences, and relationships still cause me pain today?

How do I experience these wounds physically and emotionally? What do I believe about them?

What ideal conditions do I need to heal my wounds?

Where and how do I hold shame and regret in my body? Where do I need to offer myself forgiveness?

How do I feel when I practice forgiveness of myself and others? How does it serve me?

In what areas of my life do I resist forgiving myself and others? What do I need to allow for forgiveness in these areas?

What would it feel like to release my resentments, unloving beliefs about myself, and negative energetic attachments to others?

What do I feel most ready to release right now in my life?

What shifts do I experience when I tend to my woundedness with love and compassion?

When I heal and release my wounds, what am I making space for in my life now?

Monthly Rituals

Ritual Tea
- 1 part rose petals
- 1 part lemon balm
- 1/2 part cinnamon chips

Combine all herbs in a jar or teapot; pour boiling water over herbs and steep for 20 minutes. Strain and enjoy.

Full Moon Cleansing Ritual Bath

Create a mixture of one cup Epsom or sea salt, organic rose petals (fresh or dried), a pinch of peppermint and lemon balm (fresh or dried), and a few drops of rose, rosemary and lemon essential oils. Add to a running bath along with a few tablespoons of bentonite clay for detoxing the skin.

Before entering the bath, reflect on what needs to be forgiven, released, and cleansed. Picture in your mind what true healing would look like for you in this moment. Say a prayer to Spirit (use the invocation on Page 38 or create your own), ask for cleansing and healing. As you soak in the tub, imagine the negative energy being released out of your body and into the water. Imagine the water healing your emotional and spiritual wounds. Feel your energy getting lighter. When draining the tub afterward, see all you released going down the drain. Wipe your tub out completely and dispose of the herbs left behind. Anoint yourself with your Triple Rose oil (recipe on the next page) and offer thanks to Spirit.

New Moon Candle Spell

Use a green candle, or any color that represents healing for you. Anoint your candle with oil and sprinkle with or roll in crushed rose petals and dried lemon balm. On a piece of paper, write all the emotional and spiritual wounds you are asking to be healed, speak these wounds out loud to the flame, fold the paper, and place it under the candle as it burns. Let the candle burn completely.

Candle burning safety tips: Always put your candle spell in a safe place and fire-proof container, herbs can catch fire as they burn. Do not leave burning candles unattended. If you must leave your candle unattended, put the candle in a large metal stock pot. Leave it in a bathtub or kitchen sink, away from anything flammable. For safety, please consider using small chime candles that burn quickly.

Practice: Triple Rose Self-Love Anointing Oil

This is a beautiful oil for soothing the nervous system when we do deep healing work. It embodies unconditional love and healing. Use it to celebrate and honor the gentleness of the Divine Feminine that lives in you.

In a small jar, place the following:
- Roses – love, healing, high vibration, and connection to Divine
- Chamomile flowers – healing, soothing, gentleness, calming, prosperous
- Lemon Balm – calming the nervous system and healing the body
- Rose absolute oil – healing, beauty, high vibration
- Clary Sage essential oil – calming, balancing, activating feminine desire and sensuality
- Frankincense essential oil – Divine support and love, connection to spiritual path (geranium essential oil can be substituted here)
- Rose quartz – heart healer
- Amethyst – intuition and spiritual self-discovery
- Pearls – healing, calming, soothing

Cover with oil (almond, sunflower, or light olive oil are all great options) and charge under a full moon.

How to use this anointing oil:
- Anoint your heart, belly, bottoms of your feet, and other energy centers to connect to the vibrational energy of the Divine Feminine anytime you need spiritual support, faith, trust, and to surrender.
- Dilute in a carrier oil such as almond oil or light olive oil. While your skin is still damp, use as an all-over body oil at the end of your shower. Call in self-love and healing as you do so.
- Anoint spell candles and other tools in spell work. Use in the New Moon Candle spells for each month to call in Divine love and high-vibrational energy to your intentions.
- Consecrate your magical tools—see below.

Practice: Consecrating Your Magical Tools

Throughout this book, you will make several magical tools. It is recommended that you take the time to consecrate them before using them in spells. Consecrating your tools cleanses and purifies them of residual energy and designates them for your magical work. A simple way to do this is to cleanse with smoke (burning herbs or incense) or sprinkle with salted water and anoint with an oil designed for this consecration (like the Triple Rose oil or make your own recipe). You can also call on the directions to help you consecrate your tools, connect with your ancestors for their assistance, and create your own incantation to speak over your tools to consecrate them. On Page 163, we consecrate our cauldrons for the Autumn Equinox, there you'll find step-by-step instructions for one way to consecrate your magical tools.

Celebrate Imbolc (or St. Brigid's Day)!

February 1st or 2nd in the Northern Hemisphere
August 1st or 2nd in the Southern Hemisphere

Traditionally celebrated on the 1st or 2nd of February, Imbolc is honored as the halfway point between the Winter Solstice and Spring Equinox. It is a time to say goodbye to winter and step through the portal into the energy of spring. To welcome new things, we must make room for them. This is the cycle of life, death, and rebirth. As you deepen awareness of your energy, how it impacts the cycles of your life, and how you are influenced energetically by your environment, you will gain clarity on what is ready to be cleared out, what is asking to be called in, and where boundaries and protection are needed.

The Goddess Brigid is traditionally associated with the holiday of Imbolc. She is a Gaelic Goddess of the Hearth, Protection, Fertility, and Creativity. At this threshold of spring, she is a helpful ally to connect and honor with reverence as you connect with your intentions of cleansing and protecting your home and personal energy, as well as lighting the creative spark for what you are calling in for the year ahead. You can honor her on your altar with a white candle, a cup of blessed water, and a piece of bread.

Celebrate this holiday by cleansing and protecting the energy in your home. Ask yourself:

What energy am I clearing out from winter?
What energy am I cultivating for the transition to spring?

Home cleansing rituals

Candles: Light white candles all around your home, especially on your altar, your mantle, or focal area of your main living space. Fill up your home with candlelight to clear out the darkness and heavy energy of winter and welcome the light of the returning sun.

Smoke: Light incense or burn herbs. Carry them into every room of your home, over all thresholds and windowsills, in every nook and corner. Imagine the smoke clearing your home of all negativities and any dense and residual energy from winter.

Water and Salt: Mix sea salt and fresh water in a bowl. You can add clear quartz, lemon, rosemary, or peppermint essential oils, or anything that holds the energy of cleansing and freshness to you. Use clean fingertips or a bundle of fresh herbs to sprinkle the mixture in the corners of all your rooms and across your thresholds and windowsills. While you clean, hold the intention of clearing negativity in your mind.

Sound: **Bells** are magical for shaking up energy, moving it out, and raising the vibration of a space. With the intention of clearing your space of negativity or heaviness, ring a bell around the perimeter of your home. Open your windows to let the energy move out and bring in fresh air. Afterward, play uplifting music, watch a funny TV show, make a meal you love, do something to raise your vibration, and bring positivity into your home.

Protecting your home

Mix a protective ritual salt with juniper berries and needles (cedar can also be substituted here), sea salt, and frankincense oil to sprinkle in the corners of rooms, across thresholds, and around the outside perimeter of your home or property. Call on the protection of the juniper, your guides, and ancestors to create an energetic barrier, allowing only the energies that have your permission into your sacred space.

Pentacles are also highly protective in a home space. Using your right hand, draw a pentacle in the air at every threshold and window, claiming the space lovingly and fiercely as your own, and bar any negative, heavy, unloving, or unwelcome energies from your space.

There is a spell recipe for Black Ancestral Protection Salt on Page 129; as well as a spell for creating a pentacle for your home on Page 160. Either of these can be used for home protection.

Prepare for the Next Celebration!

The Spring Equinox, also known as Ostara, is generally celebrated around March 20th in the Northern Hemisphere and September 20th in the Southern Hemisphere and is a time to honor fertility, possibility, and new growth. We celebrate this holiday by focusing our intentions (working with the element of air) and planting the seeds of what we wish to manifest for the upcoming growing season.

You may want to have on hand:
- Green, yellow, and pink candles for your altar
- Fresh flowers
- Eggs, fresh greenery, and other items to decorate your home
- A statue/depiction of the Goddess Persephone
- Your journal to record any desires or seeds you wish to plant for the growing season
- Collect items for creating a wand: branches, stones, feathers, and other adornments

Gather the items that resonate with you and are easily accessible. There is no need to purchase anything new, unless you want to! Suggested practices for Ostara are outlined in March (see Page 62).

MONTHLY REFLECTIONS

What was most challenging for me this month?

_____
_____
_____

What was most rewarding? What growth have I witnessed in myself?

_____
_____
_____

Magical associations to the Healer:

_____
_____
_____

Tree, herb, flower, and plant allies I worked with:

_____
_____
_____

Animal allies I worked with:

_____
_____
_____

Stone allies I worked with:

_____
_____
_____

Songs:

_____
_____

Scents:

_____
_____

Food and drink:

_____
_____
_____

People, Deities, Role Models:

_____
_____
_____

My Personal Practices: *What am I learning about my personal magic through these practices?*

_____
_____
_____
_____

Divine Vessel

I am a healer. I serve the Earth and the Divine Feminine. I seek healing and repair for the Divine Feminine and Masculine. I do this by seeking healing within myself and acting with intention with all things. My life is a meditation and act of gratitude to the Divine.

The Earth is Divine. She is a living breathing being, and we are part of her as a drop of salt water is to the ocean. As such, we have access to her wisdom. We are physical embodiments of her divinity. We are also limited in how we see and what we understand, so to be in service to the Divine Mother, we must be in surrender to her wisdom and guidance, even when we don't fully understand.

I am a vessel for truth and love. My vessel has been shattered through the lie of disconnection, through the debasement of the feminine, through the violence of our human system. Through spiritual devotion, I mend my vessel. With the help of my guides and ancestors, I mend my vessel. Through ceremony and celebration of the Earth, I mend my vessel. When I heal and mend my vessel, I become a pure conduit for the Divine to flow through me, manifesting its desires on the physical plane.

Chapter Three
MARCH

"I am a child of the Earth. My spirit runs wild and free."

WELCOME TO MARCH, the transition from darkness and rest to the howling, messy birthing of springtime. Our inner child lives here. With the first green shoots of spring, all raw potential and fierce desire to live, play, and claim our space in the world awakens.

Here we learn how to mother ourselves, how to hold loving space for all the hopes and dreams of our inner child. When we do this, we reclaim the genius of childhood: wildness, play, imagination, presence, and possibility. We dream again, play pretend, and talk with the fairies who live in our backyard. There is so much brilliance. Let's reclaim the gifts we have forgotten.

Wildness • Innocence • Authenticity • Imagination

The Inner Wild Child

The inner Wild Child is the little one who lives within us, who ran barefoot through the grass, and played with the fairies of the forest. They are the embodiment of innocence, pure joy, and vivid imagination. The inner Wild Child shows us gifts within us that we may have buried because of shame and the judgment of others, especially our parents and families of origin. Their connection to the Earth is pure, without the bondage of expectation and fear of abandonment.

The Wound: Parental/mother wound

The Healing: Loving and accepting the Inner Wild Child

Element: Earth/Air

Plant Ally: Motherwort
This herb is soothing and relaxing to the nervous system and the body. Use it this month to soothe the inner child when it feels unsafe, not enough, or otherwise rejecting their own unique, magical nature. When we need support, Motherwort acts as a nurturer.

Animal Ally: Deer
Deer energy embodies the nurturing aspect of the mother with the gentle, vulnerable aspect of the fawn. The mother deer must protect her fawn after birth, nursing it, and staying by its side until it is ready to venture out into the world. The fawn represents innocence and new growth, the energy of springtime.

Stone Ally: Malachite
Malachite helps us break old cycles, clears our energy, and brings gentle, supportive energy to the mind and body. With its vibrant green color, it welcomes the beginning of spring with its grounding energy. It is a powerful stone for our inner Wild Child.

Monthly Themes

Wildness: We come into this world with a natural exuberance, playfulness, and connection to the Earth that can be lost over time as we are indoctrinated into an unloving system that would prefer us to be silent and obedient. This month we will honor the wildness within us, where we access true creativity, and where we connect deeply with our instincts and intuition.

Innocence: There is so much to be valued in vulnerability, our trust in others, purity, and newness to life. Often, we fear our vulnerability and protect ourselves from being taken advantage of. It is easy to see the world as a scary place that wishes us harm. Our Inner Wild Child reclaims their birthright to innocence, to be protected and loved, and cherished just as they are.

Authenticity: The Inner Wild Child has nothing to prove to anyone. They do not question their right to be themselves in the world. They laugh when they feel joy, shed tears in their sorrow, seek comfort in their grief. One day, they are royalty, and the next day, they are a wild horse or an oyster. The Inner Wild Child honors how they feel in the moment. They do not try to hide their true self to please others.

Imagination: From places of wildness, innocence, and authenticity; imagination and creativity thrive. You are becoming, forming yourself, and always changing and evolving. This process requires you to dream into what and who you want to become. The Inner Wild Child is excited for something new, excited to learn something about themselves, try on a different way of being to see how it fits. The Inner Wild Child imagines and creates worlds through art, play, dance, stories, and any medium that suits. In honoring your raw creativity, you begin to imagine what magic can be woven into your life, outside the realm of your own self-imposed limitations.

Affirmations

I love and accept myself just as I am.

I am always growing and learning.

I am free. I am wild. I am magical.

I am worthy and lovable.

My personal affirmations:

_____

_____

_____

_____

Daily Invocation

Spirit, today I embrace my wild nature. Help me hear the voice of my inner wild child and trust in their wisdom. I call on playfulness and authenticity to help me honor my highest path and walk in joy and freedom. Unlock my imagination to envision a life filled with magic, play, and delight. Help me be fully present to this day. Help me hold my vulnerability like a precious gift, bring me love in every space. Blessed Be.

My personal intentions and prayers:

_____

_____

_____

_____

_____

_____

_____

Safe Space Meditation

Ground your breath into your body. Let your focus shift inward. Relax your muscles as you breathe and root the breath down into the Earth. Invite your higher self to support you during this meditation. Imagine walking down a path in a forest, noticing the trees and animals around you. Breathe in the crisp, fresh air and feel it in your lungs. As you walk, the forest ends, and you come into a clearing. In this clearing is a beautiful, sacred, safe space for you. It can be a place you've been to before or a place from your imagination. It can be a garden, ocean, cabin, anywhere you feel perfectly calm, safe, at home, and peaceful. Notice all the details of this sacred place. Notice everything you feel in your body here. Nothing is allowed in or out of this space without your explicit permission. It is only for you and only meant to support your well-being.

Once you have established this place in your mind's eye, invite your inner child. Notice what they look like, what they are wearing, what expression is on their face, and what they are feeling. Notice what happens inside of you when you see your inner child. How do you want to interact with them? Allow your instincts to guide you.

What does your inner Wild Child want to show you? What do they need from you right now? How can you offer them safety in this space? Take time to sit with your inner Wild Child to get to know them well. Be a loving witness to them without judgment or criticism. What do you want to say to them? What do you want your inner child to know?

When this exchange feels complete, take your little one into your arms in a loving embrace. Send them golden light of unconditional love from your heart to theirs. See your inner Wild Child receiving your light and being filled with it. Now, create a special space here in this sacred clearing that is just for your little one. Is it a fort, a tree house, a waterfall? Make your inner Wild Child something that brings them great joy and awakens their wonder and innocence. Take time to play with your little one in this place. Provide for them everything they need and want. Let them know this is their place now. They get to decide who joins them and what they do here. Tell your inner child that they are always safe and protected here.

When this feels complete, send gratitude to this sacred, safe place. Send gratitude to the Earth, your inner Wild Child, your adult self, and your higher self. Imagine a protective shield over this place before leaving it. Know you can come back here anytime you feel fearful or unsafe.

Reflections on this meditation:

CARD SPREAD

-1-
What influence does my inner Wild Child have on me today?

-2-
What parts of my child-self need love and healing?

-3-
How can I activate and honor the inner Wild Child within me?

-4-
What does my inner Wild Child want to teach me?

Journal Prompts:

Choose one or more of these questions each week to reflect and explore here or in your journal.

What is my relationship to my inner Wild Child? What thoughts, feelings, and sensations do I experience when I reflect on my inner wild child?

What times in my childhood did I feel most free and wild? When did I feel safe and loved?

What times in my childhood did I feel fear, sadness, or loneliness? What messages did I internalize about these times?

Where does my inner Wild Child need healing and unconditional love? How can I offer it to them?

What did I love to do as a child?

What kind of life did I wish for myself as a child?

What brought me the most joy and happiness in my childhood?

What gifts does my inner Wild Child carry? How can I honor these gifts today?

What would I tell my child self if they were here in front of me?

What do I love and admire about them? What is one thing I can do to let them know how much I love them?

Monthly Rituals

Ritual Tea

- 2 parts chamomile
- ½ part peppermint
- ½ part lavender
- 1 part motherwort
- ½ part marshmallow root
- 1 part lemon balm

Combine all herbs in a jar or teapot. Pour boiling water over the herbs and steep for 20 minutes. Strain. Add honey and enjoy. *Optional:* pour over ice, and have a tea party with the fairies!

Full Moon Ritual Bath

Take a cup of Epsom or sea salt and add dried motherwort, chamomile flowers, and peppermint. Light pink candles for self-love. Add your salt mixture to the bath. Add a few drops of Triple-Rose oil (See Page 44) to the water. Play music that you loved as a child to honor your inner Wild Child as you bathe.

New Moon Candle Spell

Use a pink candle and anoint it with Triple Rose oil (See Page 44). Roll in or sprinkle on an herb mixture of motherwort, chamomile, and peppermint. If you like, add rose petals to amplify self-love. Write a blessing to your inner Wild Child and speak it to the flame, include:

- What I love about you is...
- What I wish for you is...
- How I will care for you, includes...
- Help me remember...

Let the candle burn down all the way.

Practice: Unbinding Spell

As children, we have been controlled, shamed, manipulated, and dominated to be pawns of this system that does not truly love or honor us. So many of us were objectified, used, mistreated, and taken advantage of. We were made to feel unloved, unworthy, and invisible. Our Wildness was repressed and hidden to stay safe. This spell is to release the hold this programming had on you and undo the years of cultural expectations that have shaped your neural programming, and allow you freedom to be and act as you wish, authentically and brilliantly *you*.

For this ritual, you will need:
Four roses (representing you as body/Earth, mind/Air, heart/Water, and spirit/Fire)
Red yarn
Scissors/ceremonial knife

I recommend doing this ritual on the full moon, and it is fine to do it whenever works best for you. Use your wand or sprinkle salt to cast a protective circle (see Page 64) and do a grounding meditation, calling on the Earth, your guides, and higher self. Take your roses in your right hand and say: "I am this, and this is me" three times. Wrap the roses several times with the red yarn. Each time you wrap, state any roles that are binding and limiting you, any way of being that feels programmed into you and is not authentic—any feelings, behaviors, or beliefs that keep you from feeling free, wild, and powerful. Wrap the string around the roses as many times as you need to address all your current blockages.

Now take your knife or scissors and begin to cut the thread. As you do, say:
I unbind myself from all unloving and limiting roles I have taken on in this lifetime and all my lifetimes. I break all contracts that keep me small, confined, and obligated to put the needs and desires of others before my own. I release all expectations of who I think I "should" be, and now I trust that who I am is perfect and worthy to shine in my own unique brilliance. I unbind myself from guilt and free myself from the "victim" label. I fully claim my power. I am completely free and sovereign to live my life the way I see fit. Blessed Be.

When you are done cutting the threads, burn them and bury or dispose of the threads away from your home. With the roses that are left, create an altar to yourself and your new-found freedom. Work with amethyst, clear quartz, and carnelian, or any stone that resonates with your personal power. Place an image of a supportive Goddess or any deity. Lilith is a good choice to help you embody this power since she casted off her role as mate to Adam and forged her own way.

For the next 14 days from the full moon to the new moon, visit your altar. Drop into gratitude for yourself and your helpers in releasing you from your binding and allow yourself to feel the energetic freeing sensation of throwing off those old, limiting roles. Visualize yourself stepping into your power and feel your energy expanding as you do this. On the new moon, bury your flowers in a sacred spot as an offering to the Earth—offer gratitude for the support of spirit and yourself, and gratitude for the process of healing and transformation.

Celebrate the Spring Equinox (also called Ostara)!

March 20th or 21st in the Northern Hemisphere
September 20th or 21st in the Southern Hemisphere

The Spring Equinox marks the true beginning of spring, where light and darkness are in balance and seeds of intention are planted for the year ahead. It is the perfect time to think more concretely about what you want to manifest for the year. Take time to journal your ideas. The magic you weave in the coming months will assist you in bringing your vision forward into reality.

Persephone is a Greek Goddess often associated with spring. Honor her because she is also a Goddess of the Underworld, and so she holds a duality that lives in all of us: innocence, youth, and light, as well as darkness, maturity, and wisdom through experience. In the spring, Persephone rises out of the Underworld to return to our world, and help the crops grow and ripen to an abundant harvest. Fresh, new beginnings come only after a time of darkness (fall and winter), when we have cleared away what is dead and no longer viable, embraced the dreamtime of deep rest and inner journeying, and integrated the harvest and learning from the previous season.

Springtime embodies the element of air, ideas, inspiration, thoughts, expansiveness, and fresh beginnings. Here are some suggestions to work with the element of Air:

Season: Spring

Element: Air

Tarot: Suit of Swords

Direction: East

Time of day: Sunrise

Symbology: Wildness, authenticity, innocence, and imagination

Body: Mind, thoughts, and breath

Magical tools: Wind, breath, smoke, and feathers

When we work with the astral plane, we use air magic by putting thoughts and ideas out to the universe with clear intentions. Our thoughts, our words, and our choice of language have incredible magical powers.

Different types of Air magic:
Writing down your intentions and speaking them to the wind
Using daily mantras and affirmations
Creating Sigils (symbols that represent your intentions)
Using smoke to send intentions to spirit
Using wands and/or feathers to focus, direct, and move intentions
Sending intentions into the world through the breath

Meditate on your relationship to the element of air. Journal for deeper reflection:

How would you describe your relationship with the element of air—is it a soft breeze through the trees, or a hurricane?

What inspires you?

How do you connect and listen to the wisdom of your Divine self?

How does your mind work? Is it like a hamster on a wheel, spinning and hard to slow down or rein in? Or does it get easily overwhelmed, frozen, and shut down?

How can you be more intentional about your thoughts, your words, and the stories you tell of yourself?

For the Spring Equinox, we will create a wand, a tool to focus and direct your thoughts and intentions with clarity and power.

Crafting a wand

A wand is a tool of air that focuses our desires and intentions and directs them where we want them to go. Wands can cast a circle of protection and create a sacred space to hold intentions for spell work and ritual. Your wand can be as simple or elaborate as you like. To make your wand, during a time in nature find a branch or stick that calls to you. Ideally the branch is already separated from its tree of origin, but you can harvest a branch if you have a relationship with the tree, and it gives you permission to do so.

Once you've chosen your branch, take note of the type of tree it comes from and do some research into its historical magical associations. If there's a certain type of tree that you already have an intuitive or magical connection with, that may be a good place to start. Notice how your chosen wand feels in your hand. What shifts in your own energy when you hold it? Notice what energy comes from the branch (it's okay if the ability to sense energy feels new to you. This is part of the practice).

Take your wand home and do a meditation with it. Cleanse it with sacred smoke. Ask how it would like to work with you. Let it know how you would like to work with it. Take time to look at every detail and feel into how it would like to be shaped or adorned. Here are some ideas for shaping or adorning your wand:

- Leave it just as it is
- Sand it down to make it smooth
- Rub it with oil
- Make a handle by winding a strip of leather or cloth at the bottom and gluing it into place
- Add crystals or sacred stones, and/or feathers (fastening them with twine or glue)

When it's complete, you can speak your intentions into it, charge it in the full moon or sunlight, anoint it with your Triple Rose oil, and begin working with it to cast circles for ceremony or spell work.

My wand

Type of wood and its meaning to me: _____

Any additions and their meanings: _____

My intention/desire in how I will work with my wand and how it will work for me:

_____

_____

_____

How to cast a circle

When doing spell work and ceremonies, creating a sacred container is recommended. This holds the energy of your ceremonial intention inside the circle, while keeping out outside influences, energies, and distractions. Casting a circle amplifies your focus, and the magic you do is clean and pure. Your circle also recruits the assistance of the element of the Earth, so your magic is supported and balanced.

Begin by designating the area of your circle. You can do this with stones, candles, salt, herbs, or by drawing a circle around you with your wand. Ground your energy into the Earth and feel your roots expanding down. Connect with the energy of the Earth and ask for her support with thanks.

It is traditional to call in the directions from the East, though some folks start with the West or North. This is your magic and practice, you get to decide what works best. Whichever direction you start with, continue clockwise in your circle until you've called in all the directions (East-South-West-North). Feel free to play with the wording and themes so they resonate most deeply for you.

I invite the spirit of the East, the season of Spring, the element of Air, the time of Dawn. East is the Mind, beginnings, inspiration, expansion, the rising Sun, and new birth. I ask for your assistance in my work here today to bring fresh ideas and Divine vision to my circle. I thank you and honor you.

I invite the spirit of the South, the season of Summer, the element of Fire, the time of Midday. South is passion and desire, action, creativity, play, innocence, transformation, and childhood. I ask for your assistance in my work here today to bring the spark of passion and serve as a catalyst to change whatever is ready to be transformed. I thank you and honor you.

I invite the spirit of the West, the season of Autumn, the element of Water, the time of Dusk. West is emotion, introspection, receptivity, intuition, maturity. I ask for your assistance in my work here today to bring the healing balm of water and the messages of my emotions to guide me as I deepen in my understanding of myself. I thank you and honor you.

I invite the spirit of the North, the season of Winter, the element of Earth, the time of Midnight. North is the Body, our ancestors, ancient wisdom, stillness, and the fallow time. I ask for your assistance to be still and rest deeply, and to be open to the wisdom of those who have gone before me. I thank you and honor you.

I invite all my guides and angels, all my ancestors who are walking with me in the spirit realm, supporting my highest and best expression in this life. I ask for your assistance today to guide and encourage me, and show me the way when I may not see the next steps. I thank you and honor you.

Conduct your spell or ceremony. Upon completion, close your circle:

I release the spirit of the North. Stay if you will, go if you must. I honor you. Thank you and farewell.
I release the spirit of the West. Stay if you will, go if you must. I honor you. Thank you and farewell.
I release the spirit of the South. Stay if you will, go if you must. I honor you. Thank you and farewell.
I release the spirit of the East. Stay if you will, go if you must. I honor you. Thank you and farewell.
I release my spirit guides, helpers, and ancestors. Stay if you will, go if you must. I honor you. Thank you and farewell.
And so it is. The circle is closed, but never broken. Blessed Be.

Monthly Reflections

What was most challenging for me this month?

_____
_____
_____

What was most rewarding? What growth have I witnessed in myself?

_____
_____
_____

Magical associations to the Wild Child:

_____
_____
_____

Tree, herb, flower, and plant allies I worked with:

_____
_____
_____

Animal allies I worked with:

_____
_____
_____

Stone allies I worked with:

_____
_____
_____

Songs:

_____
_____

Scents:

_____
_____

Food and drink:

_____
_____
_____

People, Deities, Role Models:

_____
_____
_____

My Personal Practices: *What am I learning about my personal magic through these practices?*

_____
_____
_____
_____

Home

There is a rift in my heart. It lays between myself and my home. I feel the longing for it, not knowing where it is exactly.

Florida, the land where I was born.
Swampy and damp,
Mosquitoes rising out of sandy hills
My mother was raised here; poor and motherless herself
In a greyhound bus. A servant to her father
Feeding the chickens
Sorrow in the soil pressed between her bare feet.

Virginia, the land where I was raised.
Beautiful mountains and twisting rivers
History.
The history of very important men deciding how things should be
Pride in the forming of a nation that enslaves, oppresses, and takes land through lies, deception, and force. Revolution. Genocide. Civil War.
Racist.
Put me in my place more times than I can count:
Be silent. Be beautiful.
Be pleasing. Be submissive.
And art and theater and Edgar Allen Poe and childhood play in forests with magic
Fireflies.

West Virginia
Where I came into myself
Got chewed up and spit out
But also loved
Saw what was possible for my life:
A country home
An artist's studio
Powerful women living unapologetically among
The farmers and country boys
Who would force you if they could
So, I learned to say NO loudly and often
And I learned to love the river
And paint myself with clay by grinding the colorful rocks

Resting on the river bottom
And I learned to love the land
Rolling endlessly, mists rising
Holding the secrets of its magic that you can only get to
down that holler
Through the raspberry brambles
In the abandoned church
Where an old man shows you how to hold a banjo and pluck its strings
A simple melody
With a million layers of meaning

And Oregon now
High desert
Birds of prey and twisted junipers
A land of migrants living freely and Natives on reservations
Epic sunsets over rising volcanoes
White folks creating their utopia...pushing Brown and Black bodies into the shadows
And Brown and Black folks rising, raising their voices to heal the trauma of generations.
More twisting rivers, tumbling over lava beds, fed from alpine lakes
Hot springs, horses, acres and acres of alfalfa.

The lands of my ancestors also call:
Wales, Scotland, Germany, Italy
I do not know these lands.
But my blood remembers and yearns to return.

And I realize I am a nomad.
My home is me.
My home is my memories of boys I've loved
and girls, too.
And meandering paths to swimming holes deep in the mountain
And a warm coffee shop that smells of roasting beans and tobacco
And circling around a maypole
And towering volcanoes
And a million tears for the places I've lost, for the
longing in my heart for a place that is mine.
I am mine.
I am my home.

CHAPTER FOUR
APRIL

"My body is sacred. I bring beauty into the world."

APRIL IS OFTEN the time to celebrate Easter, a time of potent rebirth and resurrection. The Earth is coming back to life! It is a time of possibilities, the buds have not fully bloomed, and the promise of them is enough to ignite our excitement for the coming of warmer days and fertile growth. This month we are invited to tend and nourish our inner soil in the places we want things to grow. The themes of the Maiden will assist in this work.

Desire ✦ Pleasure ✦ Joy ✦ Beauty

The Maiden

The Maiden archetype is a young woman growing into her power, learning about pleasure and desire, connecting with her unique magic as an embodiment of the Divine Feminine. The energy of manifestation is one of delightful receiving, joyful anticipation, celebrating what is and what is to come. This begins with loving ourselves, just as we are. It is marveling in the miracle of our bodies, hearts, minds, and wombs. It is experiencing the beauty of spring blossoming with fire in our bellies, giving and receiving pleasure under a ripening sun. The Maiden shows us exactly how to worship our Divine beauty through desire and pleasure. When we do so, we claim a life of alignment, joy, and personal power.

The Wound: Self-hatred

The Healing: Self-worship

Element: Air

Plant Ally: Calendula
Calendula is a beautiful yellow flower, evoking sun energy and lighting up our lives. It is also very soothing and healing for the body, particularly to the skin. Work with it in infused oils and beauty products to worship ourselves and our miraculous physical vessels.

Animal Ally: Butterfly
The butterfly represents beauty, but it has navigated a harrowing journey to embody such beauty. This honors the path of the Maiden so many of us have walked: the transformation of embodying our beauty, femininity, and magic requires a loss of our old selves and stories, particularly those attached to who we were as young people. Butterflies are alchemized through the chrysalis to help us become the highest expressions of ourselves—magical creatures that inspire awe wherever we go. *Yes* we are perfect just the way we are *and* are always changing and transforming into something new and magical.

Stone Ally: Amethyst
I find amethyst to be one of the most beautiful crystals and a potent ally for the inner Maiden. This stone helps us access our inner power and balance our moods to bring a steady, loving presence to our spiritual work.

Monthly Themes

Desire: In Judeo-Christian traditions, feminine desire is portrayed as evil, shameful, dirty, and dangerous. No wonder we have internalized these feelings in our bodies to obstruct our connection to desire. For we have been programmed to believe that what we want is inherently bad. Feminine sexuality has been so tightly controlled because it is so powerful. When these belief systems are dismantled, we become instruments of the Divine, creating the world through us, with desire as the guide.

Pleasure is the sensation of bringing desire into form. It is a very potent frequency for manifestation. Feeling pleasure can be scary if you have been programmed to always be vigilant to the threat of harm. You must feel safe in your body to experience pleasure. To feel safe, you must feel held, protected, and loved. If you have trauma in your body, your brain will register pleasure as danger, and your fight or flight response will kick in to make sure you don't feel too good. Our culture has associated pleasure with the narrative "she was asking for it," by reminding us of our flaws, activating our shame, and shutting down our ability to experience pleasure. Experiencing pleasure is something that must be cultivated and can be done daily, in small and powerful ways, reclaiming your Divine right to feel delight in your body.

Beauty is a natural law of the universe. We see this in the Earth around us, as a rose blossoms fragrantly in summer, in majestic sun rises and sun sets, in the magic of the moon and stars and galaxies, and in our glorious bodies, our curves and lines, the sparkle in our eyes, the softness of our skin, the way we change the energy of our day by how we adorn ourselves. This is not about conforming to "conventional" ideas of beauty (though that's fine if you do); this is about reclaiming our own ideas of what is beautiful and celebrating the infinite ways beauty is manifested on our planet. When we celebrate and cultivate beauty in our lives, we open ourselves to receive beauty in the form of love, connection, joy, and expansiveness.

Joy is the natural result of being aligned with our desires, pleasure, and personal concept of beauty. It is what happens when we create a world that is in service to our highest path, aligned with Spirit. When we soften and open our hearts to receive the gifts of the Earth every day, joy flows through us like a fountain. It is found in the little things, like a baby's smile or a gentle breeze, a shooting star, and a delicious meal. Stop putting off your joy. How often do you find yourself saying, "When XYZ happens, then I'll be happy?" Find and claim it right now! When you do, you align with the frequency to cultivate more of it. When you put it off, you are restricting the flow of joy that is available to you.

Affirmations:

My body is sacred.

I receive pleasure freely and abundantly.

I bring beauty into the world.

Joy is my Divine birthright.

My personal affirmations:

_____
_____
_____
_____

Daily Invocation

Spirit, today I welcome desire as guidance for the life I am creating for myself. I love myself deeply and trust that my desires will lead me to the experiences of pleasure and joy today. I know my experience of pleasure and joy creates more space for others to experience them as well. I cultivate beauty in all my actions. I honor the beauty in myself, as a Divine creation. Help me release all blocks to aligning with my Divine desires, pleasure, beauty, and joy. Blessed be.

My personal intentions and prayers:

_____
_____
_____
_____
_____
_____
_____
_____

Worshipping the Maiden Meditation

Begin by grounding into your breath, sending your breath down into the Earth. Call on your higher self for support during this meditation. Imagine a beautiful place in nature, like a clearing in a grove of trees, with a beautifully adorned altar in the center of the clearing. Call forth your inner wise woman/higher self. See her looking lovingly in your eyes with her arms open, welcoming you into a loving embrace. Feel her unconditional love and acceptance fill your heart space, as your hearts beat together. Then, call forth your inner maiden. See her coming forward as both you and your wise woman welcome her into a loving embrace, filling her with unconditional love and acceptance. Now, lay your maiden on the altar, surrounded with flowers, candles, and incense. Call forth your guides, angels, and ancestors. See them surrounding your maiden, as you and your wise woman put your hands on each of her shoulders, the rest of your guides put their hands on her as well, sending her love and acceptance. Feel yourself as the maiden, receiving this beautiful unconditional love, understanding deeply that you are perfect exactly the way you are. Offer gratitude to your guides, the Earth, and yourself.

Reflections on this meditation:

Card Spread

-1-
What is my relationship to my inner maiden right now?

-2-
What is being asked of me to heal the relationship with my inner maiden?

-3-
In order to bring more pleasure, joy, and beauty into my life, what must I release?

-4-
What message does my inner maiden have for me?

Journal Prompts

Choose one or more of these questions each week to reflect and explore here or in your journal.

What is my relationship to desire and pleasure? What thoughts, feelings, or sensations arise when I reflect on these concepts?

What messages did I receive and internalize about desire and pleasure as a young person?

How do these influence my ability to access my pleasure and desire in my life now?

What do I desire? What brings me pleasure?

What were my experiences of desire, pleasure, and joy as a young person (age 12 into my 20s)? What was supportive of my growth? What was harmful?

What did my Maiden-self need and not receive? How can I offer it to her now?

What do I love most about myself?

Where is there beauty in my life right now? How can I cultivate more of this?

What brings me joy in my life right now? How can I cultivate more of this?

Monthly Rituals

Ritual Tea

- 1 part calendula flowers
- 1 part meadowsweet herb
- ½ part lavender
- ½ part rosehips

Combine all herbs in a jar or teapot; pour boiling water over herbs and steep for 20 minutes. Strain.

Full Moon Ritual Bath

Run a bath and add the following:
- A cup of milk
- A handful of calendula flowers (dried or fresh)
- A few drops of patchouli essential oil
- A couple tablespoons almond or light olive oil

As you soak in this soothing bath, take time to meditate on the parts of yourself that you see as beautiful. See the sun energy of the calendula flowers lighting up the joy in all of your cells. Feel it radiating out of your heart and into the world, with the water amplifying the effects around you. Allow yourself to receive the loving and soothing effects of this healing bath.

New Moon Candle Spell

Use a golden-colored candle. Anoint with oil and roll in or sprinkle on honey and dried calendula flowers or petals. Speak your intentions to the candle as you light it on your altar. Use the invocation on Page 73 or create your own to call on healing and love for your inner maiden.

Practice: Honoring the Maiden through Self-worship

These are recommended to do along with your Ritual Bath to deeply honor your inner Maiden.

Healing and calming body scrub and face mask

Combine one tablespoon of dried, powdered calendula flowers with one tablespoon of raw unfiltered honey. This is the base for the body scrub and face mask below.

Body scrub

Take one tablespoon of the calendula and honey mixture and add:

- Two tablespoons of sea salt
- Two tablespoons of almond or light olive oil

Mix well and apply in the bath. Rub into skin starting with the feet and working up all the way to the throat. Rinse well.

Face mask

Use one tablespoon of the calendula and honey mixture and add:

- One tablespoon plain full fat yogurt
- One teaspoon rolled oats, ground to a fine powder (optional)

Mix well and apply to a clean face and throat. Allow to dry on skin for 10–15 minutes, then rinse thoroughly.

Practice: Vision Board

Vision Boards are simple and powerful spells to call in what you desire. This is how we begin to cultivate our Dream Seed into the physical realms—the seeds of our desire and what is being created through you. You will need:

- A piece of poster board, whatever size you like
- Magazines, photos, old greeting cards
- Scissors and glue

As you engage with your inner Maiden this month, tune into the sensation of desire. What do you desire most for yourself in your life? What do you desire five years from now? Ten years from now? Take time to meditate and journal on this to gain clarity for the kind of life that will bring you pleasure, how it would look and feel to you. Ask your guides to help give you clarity about what you are meant to do, be, and experience in this life in love, beauty, joy, and abundance. Take note of images, sensations, and emotions that come up.

Look through magazines and images. Without thinking too much about exactly what you are looking for, pick out whatever strikes you. Allow your intuition to guide you. Cut out all the images that resonate with you. Then begin to arrange them on your poster board, all the while feeling into the energy of expansion and creation. Glue the magazine pieces on however you like, and don't feel obligated to use every single image you cut out. Save the rest for future vision boards!

When your vision board is complete, display it in a place where you will see it every day: on the wall by your bed, on your bathroom mirror, or at your altar. When you look at it, let yourself drop into the energetic flow of the feeling it evokes for you. This is how you get into energetic alignment with your desire and allow it to manifest in your life.

Prepare for the Next Celebration!

Walpurgisnacht or Beltane is celebrated on April 30th or May 1st in the Northern Hemisphere and October 31 or November 1 in the Southern Hemisphere. We celebrate this holiday as a fire festival and the gateway to summer.

You may want to have on-hand:

- Candles of all colors, particularly orange and red
- Colorful ribbons to decorate your altar, home space, and outdoor spaces
- Jasmine or patchouli scented incense
- A space to have a gathering around a fire
- Anything you have that can represent the welcoming of summer, fire season, passion, desire, and celebrations!

Monthly Reflections

What was most challenging for me this month?

_____
_____
_____

What was most rewarding? What growth have I witnessed in myself?

_____
_____
_____

Magical associations with the Maiden:

_____
_____
_____

Tree, herb, flower, and plant allies I worked with:

_____
_____
_____

Animal allies I worked with:

_____
_____
_____

Stone allies I worked with:

___
___
___

Songs:

___
___
___

Scents:

___
___
___

Food and drink:

___
___
___

People, Deities, Role Models:

___
___
___

My Personal Practices: *What am I learning about my personal magic through these practices?*

___
___
___
___

Ode to My Body

My body is a Cauldron
when the moon is new
myths and secrets dance with desire,
conjuring the ability
to dream one's dreams

My body is the Goddess
succulent wild woman
cinnamon, nutmeg, salt, and clove
Queen of hearth and temple
playful
powerful
revered wisdom
and glowing fervor

My body is a Witness
while we turn on the music
the magic of our plump
friendly figures
matures and is harvested
to sacred repose
when the moon is full.
quiet.
unabashed.

My body is a Lover
laughing soulmate
serenely sauntering
obtaining the fruit
of immortal morsels
flooded with candlelight

My body is a Healer
soul refresher
spoon the batter
inserted into the center
time to gather in the coolness of the fall
and be warmed
soul sister
with nourishing gentle counsel.

CHAPTER FIVE
MAY

"I trust my inner authority. I share my vision with the world."

IN MAY, we reflect on our relationship to authority, internal and external. This work gives us a clear picture of our strengths and limitations as we peer deeper into our inner realms. It is time to get clear on our values to better discern if we are living in alignment with them or not. When we are aligned with what matters most to us, we are more effective at "tending our gardens." In other words, we make choices to create the life that is aligned with our highest potential. As the buds burst through the soil in the spring, we see what is growing in our garden that needs to be weeded out.

Humility ✦ Integrity ✦ Discernment ✦ Accountability

The Hierophant

The Hierophant is an archetype in the Tarot of spiritual authority. In these difficult times, our relationship to authority is changing as we come into our power discern our personal truths around right and wrong. The Hierophant guides us in taking the teachings of our elders, systems, and institutions and weighs them against what's right for us. They invite us to question what we believe and why we believe it. For instance, if you were raised Christian, you are invited to see where the teachings of Christianity may continue to be an intrinsic part of your belief system, where Christianity was misused to harm or control others, and where you can lovingly challenge or let go of the more destructive elements of these ancient beliefs. The Hierophant teaches us to stand in our truth, live in alignment with our values, and always be open to learning and shifting our belief systems when they are no longer aligned with who you are.

The Wound: Rigidity and Perfectionism

The Healing: Humility

Element: Air

Plant Ally: Nettle

Nettle is an ancient, wise, and resilient plant with deep wisdom to share. This ally shows us that everything has the potential to harm (with its stinging leaves and stems) or heal (with its powerful medicinal properties). Nettle teaches us strength and gentleness, and the importance of seeing all sides of a situation before judging.

Animal Ally: Eagle

The Eagle soars high above the landscape to see the big picture. Its keen eyes detect even the smallest creatures from far away. Eagle invites us to back up and put things in perspective, and trust our vision, even if someone or something seeks to deceive us.

Stone Ally: Selenite

This is a master stone that clears its own energy and the energy of other crystals as well. Selenite is a connector to Divine wisdom and an ally in discernment—clearing out the bullshit and amplifying truth without judgment or negativity.

Monthly Themes

Humility: Perfectionism is a trap in which many of us find ourselves. The trap is often rooted in a painful belief that we are not enough as we are. Humility heals us from the pressure of having to be perfect by allowing us to be human, make mistakes, and learn from them. When things are perfect, there is no room for growth. Humility creates space for growth, so we can become the best version of ourselves in any given moment, which will continue to change. As humility gives others permission to be authentic in their humanity, it also creates safety in our relationships with others.

Integrity: People pleasing and perfectionism are barriers to living in integrity. We learn to silence our inner-knowing and live by others' values, beliefs, and expectations. Integrity is sometimes defined as "doing the right thing when no one is looking," but it is also about being true to ourselves in each moment, every choice we make, setting boundaries, and following our desires. If we value honesty but tell half-truths because we are worried what others will think, we are out of integrity. If we value the concept of "do no harm," we must be willing to look at ways we unconsciously cause harm or contribute to harmful systems and institutions. When we are acting with integrity to our values and belief systems, we are aligned, life flows more smoothly, and we manifest more effectively.

Accountability: It is important to take responsibility for our emotions, thoughts, behaviors, and impact on others. It is no one's job to fix us, heal us, or rescue us—that is an inside job. Being accountable to ourselves is an extremely empowering act, as it helps us release our stories of victimhood and "live in the solution," and actively seek what will help us resolve the areas of our life that don't feel good. If something isn't working in your life, this is an invitation to see how you may be contributing to the dynamic. For example: are you setting healthy boundaries? Speaking your truth? Honoring yourself? Are you operating out of toxic belief systems that do not support you? This type of self-examination is rooted in humility. It allows us to see where we are accountable to unloving ways of being in our relationships and choices that affect the world around us, so we can own it and make amends where necessary, or change our behaviors to be more aligned with our values.

Discernment: Sometimes it is hard to see the truth in intense dynamics and whether it is our mind deceiving us or the words and actions of others that are manipulating our thoughts. Through knowing ourselves, values, where we take responsibility and where we do not, we gain the power of discernment. When we root deeply in our inner knowing through a trusting relationship with Spirit, we decide what is best for us and what is not. We stop giving our attention and energy to that which is not of service. This is the eye of the Eagle, soaring above the horizon, able to see all elements of a situation and identify our truth in it. From there, we can choose a course of action that is right for us.

Affirmations

I release expectations of perfection in myself and others.

I am humble and open to honest self-reflection.

I live in alignment with my values.

I welcome learning in all areas of my life.

My personal affirmations:

_____
_____
_____

Daily invocation

Spirit, I humbly come with gratitude for your teaching and guidance on my path. Help me be aligned with what truly matters to me. Today I take responsibility for my actions without fear, shame, or guilt. Show me how to learn with humility. Show me how to walk in integrity on my highest path and with the Earth and all beings. Show me where I am a teacher to others and help me role model responsible and loving authority. Give me discernment to identify what is and is not in service to the liberation of the collective and myself.

My personal intentions and prayers:

_____
_____
_____
_____
_____
_____
_____
_____

Inner Teacher Meditation

Begin by grounding in your breath. Bring awareness to your body. Notice how you feel. Where you are holding tension? Send loving breath to these places. Root your energy down into the Earth and ask your higher self for support during this meditation. Imagine yourself in a beautiful sacred temple. A place of learning and wisdom. Feel your energy as you walk inside, taking note of all you see. It is a place you have visited before in the spirit realm. Allow it to feel like a welcome home. Notice two beautiful golden doors opening to a great hall. As you step through the doors, you see all your teachers standing before you. Every schoolteacher, religious and spiritual teacher, your family members, professors, and role models from this life. Take a moment to look at each one. Notice which teachers supported your highest path, and which ones were allowed to lead you astray. Take note that each one guided you and taught you something about yourself. Notice if there are feelings of pain, resentment, or betrayal present. Feel the sacred power of the temple absorbing these feelings and replacing them with higher understanding and gratitude for what you learned in these relationships. Offer forgiveness and release the shame of not knowing. Notice if there are feelings of excitement, love, or connection with your teachers. Offer gratitude for the love and support. Ask these teachers to continue to walk with you on your path.

As you stand in this temple room, feel the deep knowledge that you are also a teacher; each of these people have learned something from you as well. Notice how that feels in your body. Do you feel like the teacher you want to be? If not, pay attention to what you would like to do differently moving forward in your life. What do you want to role model? What values do you wish to uphold for others to see? Feel any shame or regret around this also being dissolved and transformed into gratitude for these potent lessons.

When you feel complete, send love and gratitude to all your teachers and turn to leave the room. The golden doors now lead out to a beautiful garden. Waiting at the threshold is a majestic golden Eagle. The Eagle looks at you with sharp eyes. You know Eagle has been waiting for you. The Eagle spreads its wings, inviting you to climb on its back. As you do, it soars into the sky, high above the temple and beautiful gardens. The Eagle takes you over forests and rivers, mountains and meadows, showing you the vast beauty of the Earth beneath you. As you fly, you understand the truth that you are your greatest teacher, and the whole world is reflecting your truth back to you. Excitement courses through your body. You know in your bones the power of your beliefs and intentions. You receive the profound beauty of all that is around you. You offer gratitude to the Eagle and the Earth for its wisdom.

The Eagle brings you back to Earth, returning you to your meditation space. Offer it a loving goodbye and watch it fly away, knowing it is always here to help you gain perspective when you need it. Feel the lessons filling your cells. Take a deep cleansing breath and return your awareness to your body and the room around you. You are complete.

Reflections on this meditation:

Card Spread

-1-
Where am I out of alignment with my values?

-2-
What action can I take to align with my values?

-3-
How is Spirit supporting me to find this alignment?

-4-
What am I learning in this process?

Journal Prompts

Choose one or more of these questions each week to reflect and explore here or in your journal.

What is coming up for me around the themes of humility, integrity, and accountability in my life now?

How does alignment feel in my body? What does it feel like when I am out of alignment?

Who are some of my most impactful teachers? What have they taught me about accountability and integrity, both positive and negative?

What is my relationship to perfectionism? What was I taught about it growing up?

How did I internalize the lessons of perfectionism, humility, integrity, accountability, and discernment?

What traits do I consider my weaknesses? What traits do I consider my strengths?

What thoughts, feelings, and sensations arise when I examine my strengths and weaknesses?

The top 10 values I identify with in my life are...

How do these values manifest in my life? Where in my life am I acting out of alignment with these values?

What does it feel like when I act out of alignment with these values? What choices can I make to live more in alignment with my values in my life right now?

Monthly Rituals

Ritual Tea

Spring Re-mineralizing Tea:
- 1 part holy basil (tulsi)
- 1 part red clover herb
- 1 part nettle leaf
- 1 part oatstraw
- 1 part raspberry leaf

Combine all herbs in a jar or teapot. Pour boiling water over the herbs. Steep for 20 minutes. Strain and enjoy.

Full Moon Ritual Bath

Make an herbal infusion by pouring boiling water over nettle, peppermint, and dandelion flowers (fresh or dried) and allow it to infuse for at least one hour, then strain. Add the infusion to a warm bath with one cup of sea salt or Epsom salt. For a more uplifting effect, add a couple of drops of eucalyptus essential oil.

New Moon Candle Spell

Use a blue or white candle, anoint with oil and sprinkle on or roll in salt and dried nettle leaves. Use with the Sigil spell described in the next section.

Practice: Sigils

Sigils are air magic, associated with higher wisdom, the mind, and clear, focused intention. They are symbols of our intentions that are sent to Spirit. You can create sigils for any intention you have. Sigils are incredibly powerful, so I recommend using discernment and prudence when casting them.

This sigil spell is designed to help clarify the values and principles you choose to live by at this time and claim alignment with them. When you are out of alignment, Spirit will help you get back on track. I recommend doing this spell with your New Moon candle spell this month.

To create the sigil:

For a general sigil: write your intention for what you want to call in, manifest, or create. Imagine your want or desire is already here. Write your want or desire in the present tense, using positive language For example, instead of, *"I'm not afraid."* Put it in its positive form, *"I am courageous."* Do not use negatives like not, aren't, can't, won't, and don't.

For this sigil, write an intention around how you choose to align with what matters most to you in your personal work and in your magic. Look to your journal writings on your values for guidance. For instance, if your values are community, integrity, and self-love, your statement could be: "I am living in deep integrity, honoring and loving myself in all my actions. I am a positive contributor to the highest good of my community, aligned in my thoughts and actions."

Once your intention is written, create a symbol that represents your intention. There are many ways to do this. Here are two, but use your intuition or check the Resources section on Page 218.

For a "freestyle" sigil: Make a symbol that embodies the energy of your intention. When you see the symbol, it evokes feelings of your intention becoming actualized.

For a more structured approach to your sigil: Look at your written intention and cross out all vowels and repeating letters. Keep letters that do not repeat (for instance, for the statement above "I am courageous", the non-repeating letters are m, c, r, g, and s). Create a symbol from these letters, until it feels right to you.

Draw your sigil on a fresh piece of paper. Light a candle on your altar, with a fireproof bowl handy (or you can do this with fire in your fireplace or outside). Hold the energy of your intention in your mind's eye and your piece of paper in your right hand. Feel the energy of your intention building. When you're ready, burn the sigil with the candle flame over the fireproof bowl. See the smoke rising to Spirit—the energy of your intention transforming with the element of Fire. Trust your intention or desire is coming to you now. Give thanks.

Celebrate Walpurgisnacht/Beltane!

April 30th or May 1st in the Northern Hemisphere
October 31st or November 1st in the Southern Hemisphere

Walpurgisnacht is traditionally celebrated on the last night of April and Beltane is celebrated from sunset on April 30th to sunset on May 1st. This is the threshold between Spring and Summer, a fire festival to celebrate fertility and growth. In Germany and other parts of Europe, Walpurgisnacht is a night when witches ride on their brooms to the Brocken—a peak in the Harz Mountains of Central Germany—to dance around the fire and weave their magic.

Frau Holle, a Germanic goddess also known as "the White Lady," rides on her broom, protecting unbaptized children who have died. She is also featured in a classic fairy tale where two sisters fall into a well. One sister enters her service and works hard. The other does not. Frau Holle rewards the first sister with showers of gold, and the second sister is cursed to spit out frogs whenever she tries to speak. Frau Holle teaches us about discernment, an important theme for the month of May.

During this time, reflect on your relationship to discernment in your life. Some questions for journaling:

Who do you allow into your life?

Do these relationships serve you and your highest path? Or do they lack reciprocity and drain you in some way?

How do you spend your free time? Do you spend it on things that serve you and your highest path, such as self-care, self-enrichment, and activities that bring you joy and pleasure? Or do you spend your free time on things that are not of service to you, taking too much care for others, scrolling on social media, or running yourself into the ground without rest?

How can you be more discerning in how you spend your time and energy? Who has access to you, your time, and energy?

In honor of Walpurgisnacht, we will craft a broom to help you sweep out forces in your life that are not in service to your highest good. Brooms are an important witch's tool for cleansing a space, preparing an area for ritual or ceremony, and worked with as protection when hung by a doorway or over a hearth.

Supplies needed:

- A sturdy length of wood for your handle. The length will determine the size of the broom, if you want a full-size broom, choose a piece about 4-feet long. You can make a smaller one for ease and convenience and ceremonial purposes—it will carry the same intention and magic of a larger one.
- A large stack of thinner branches, grasses, or woody herbs for your bristles. Harvest the new growth that is sprouting around this time (*please harvest with intention and permission from the plant you are choosing*). Make sure branches, grasses, or woody herbs are thin enough to bend easily but not break.
- Sturdy twine

Step 1: If needed, soak your bristles overnight in warm water to make them pliable.

Step 2: Begin with your handle and align the bristles with the bottom all around the handle, so they are pointing up toward the top of the handle (they will look like they are going backward).

Step 3: Take your twine and wrap it several times around your bristles several inches above the bottom of the handle.

Step 4: Tie it securely with the twine (you can also use glue for extra reinforcement).

Step 5: Next, bend your bristles down so they are now pointing toward the bottom of the broom, over the twine.

Step 6: Wrap the bristles and again with twine and tie off securely.

Step 7: If desired, add embellishments to your broom (wrap leather around the handle, glue or tie on crystals or charms, and more). Make your broom as simple or ornate as you like. How it looks matters only in how much it matters to you. It is perfectly acceptable to start with a simple, well-made tool for your magic. What matters most is the energy and intention you put into your broom.

Step 8: When your broom is complete, allow it to dry completely.

Step 9: Cleanse your broom with smoke or salt water, and anoint it with your Triple Rose Oil to designate it as a magical tool.

Prepare for the Next Celebration!

Summer Solstice or Litha is celebrated around June 21st in the Northern Hemisphere and December 21st or 22nd in the Southern Hemisphere. This is a time in which we honor and celebrate both the peak of summer and the beginning of the dying sun.

You may want to have on-hand:
- Red, gold, and white candles
- Red Roses
- Wine
- Dragon's Blood incense
- A beeswax candle for your Summer Solstice spell (begin to gather your supplies for this as well, listed on Page 115)
- Anything that connects you to your personal power, passion, and fire, such as clothes that make you feel powerful and sexy, poems, art, and more. Suggestions for celebrating Summer Solstice are offered for the month of June (see Page 114).

Monthly Reflections

What was most challenging for me this month?

_____
_____
_____

What was most rewarding? What growth have I witnessed in myself?

_____
_____
_____

Magical associations to the Hierophant:

_____
_____
_____

Tree, herb, flower, and plant allies I worked with:

_____
_____
_____

Animal allies I worked with:

_____
_____
_____

Stone allies I worked with:
_____
_____
_____

Songs:
_____
_____
_____

Scents:
_____
_____
_____

Food and drink:
_____
_____
_____

People, Deities, Role Models:
_____
_____
_____

My Personal Practices: *What am I learning about my personal magic through these practices?*
_____
_____
_____

Carrying the Bones

The bones are restless
rattling angrily inside
a heavy black suitcase

They scream their stories
haunting memories of
failure
betrayal
sorrow
fear.

They seek to warn me:
"you are not safe"
"god does not love you"
"you will never belong."

The screaming of my ancestors
their memories pulsing in my heart's blood
drowns out deeper truths

Four corpses
a story of place—disconnected from our ancestral lands
roaming ghosts, insatiably consuming that which is not ours
from longing

a story of burdens—carry it all yourself
know the plan, be in charge
don't make mistakes

a story of working—to exhaustion
proving our worth in tired feet
calloused hands
nothing left for ourselves

a story of abandonment—
unlovable children growing into

unlovable adults
suffocating in shame.

These bones I carry,
keep me from remembering
I am loved
I am safe
I belong where my feet touch this Earth
with reverence

I bury the bones in the sandy desert.
"Be at peace," I tell them
Rest and receive your release from this realm you have been trapped in so long
trapped in my body
trapped in our stories
trapped in patterns of disconnection, fear, abandonment

I release these patterns
I find my own truth
I no longer carry the bones
of decaying structures and lost ancestors

I carry my own truth now.
I am free.
I am at peace.

Chapter Six
JUNE

"I am sovereign. I rule over my creation."

WELCOME TO JUNE, when flowers begin to ripen into fruit. The days are getting warmer, and the light of the sun and the dynamic energy makes possible the realm of creation. Life flourishes as we move into action—from dreaming and planning to manifesting into physical form. To do this, trust yourself, surrender your limiting beliefs and programming that keep you stuck, and get comfortable overseeing your reality. This requires us to be confident in our worthiness to create the lives we wish to live—steeped in beauty, joy, and love. The heat and fire of the Summer Solstice assists us by lighting up our passion and fire for the world we are calling into being now.

Sovereignty • Freedom • Leadership • Power

The Queen

The Queen rules her life without needing permission or approval from others. She and her Higher Self are at the center of her universe. She knows that when she comes first, she has more to give to others. By speaking her truth, she leads others with humility, does not compromise her boundaries or her desires, lives authentically, and uses her power with responsibility and wisdom. She is the result of the embodiment of the other archetypes and can only exist when we've done the personal work to stand fully in our power. The Queen's focus is the intentional cultivation of a way of being that is nourishing, collaborative, respectful, and life-giving. When these are honored and in balance, the Queen leads and creates the world that we are all dreaming into being.

As we get comfortable standing in our power, we are no longer controlled or manipulated by others. When we let go of other people's visions for our lives, we break free from patterns to make ourself small, silent, invisible so others can feel less threatened by our brilliance.

The Wound: Disempowerment/self-doubt

The Healing: Empowerment/self-trust

Element: Air/Fire

Plant Ally: Lavender
A magical plant that brings beauty and balance to the soul, body, and nervous system. Lavender offers us a stable foundation to source our power and calms us when fear causes us to doubt ourselves.

Animal Ally: Lioness
The Lioness is a symbol of sheer power. Female Lions are the main hunters and organizers of the social structure of the pride. When not hunting or protecting their territory, life is relaxed and enjoyable; the Lioness understands this balance well. The Lioness shows us how to live in harmony with other powerful women and femmes, to stand in our power, and acknowledge the important contributions we make to our communities.

Stone Ally: Carnelian
For our inner queen, this is a stone of power, confidence, and energy. Work with Carnelian to give an extra boost of power and intent to your spells and rituals, or carry this stone in a pocket or in jewelry to embody your power as you move through your days.

Monthly Themes

Sovereignty is the idea that we are in complete power over ourselves and in relationship with the Divine. We make the rules, boundaries, and expectations for our lives—no one else gets to dictate what we believe, the values we live by, and the choices we make. It is a practice of examining our past experiences of victimhood and powerlessness with compassion and releasing the victim role in order to support our growth and empowerment moving forward.

Freedom is a potent concept for the times we live in. On a spiritual plane, we are all free. Today's systems have programmed us to believe we are stuck, which is not the case. When we embody freedom within ourselves—examining all options, remembering that we have choice in every action—we become empowered to see where liberation is accessible to others and ourselves. This supports the creation of systems that bring freedom to all people. You are free to put your own healing and wellness first. You are free to imagine and work toward creating the life you desire and the world you desire to live in.

Leadership is about doing your spiritual work so you can rise to create the world of tomorrow. In our current system, women, femmes, and other marginalized folks have been punished for daring to stand up as leaders. This marginalization creates a programming of fear, keeping us small to keep us safe. A Queen does not shy away from using her voice and influence to lead others. Whether we remain small and scared or take up space and speak our truth, the Queen within knows that her life influences people all the time. Queens live by example, showing others what is possible, and reflecting their brilliance back to the people around them by operating in a spirit of collaboration, not domination. New rules are created that are in alignment with what matters most to us. Parents, friends, lovers, artists, teachers, healers are all leaders in some way.

Power: When the Divine feminine is empowered, systems become collaborative and in service to the collective. The Divine feminine is not interested in amassing wealth or hoarding power. It is interested in creation, connection, and the delight that comes from experiencing desire manifested in physical form. It nurtures. It dreams. It laughs. It challenges unloving structures with a force to be reckoned with. You are a spiritual being of infinite power. When you tap into it and learn to trust it, you create anything you want. There are many things we do not have power over. This is about understanding the power we have—over our thoughts, feelings, attitudes, behaviors, language, the relationships we choose and what we call into existence. What we say *yes* or *no* to is where we focus our energy. Our choices are where our true power lies.

Affirmations

I am sovereign and free.

I release my stories of victimhood.

I claim my power.

I am limitless. All things are possible.

My personal affirmations:

_____
_____
_____
_____

Daily Invocation

Spirit, today I will trust myself. Under your guidance and support, I step into my power to create the life I want. I embrace my sovereignty. I give myself permission to say NO to anything that does not align for me. I give myself permission to say YES to my desires. I weave the world around me through my thoughts, feelings, stories, and actions. Let my inner world align with my highest path. Let me create a world around me filled with love, beauty, and joy. Blessed Be.

My personal intentions and prayers:

_____
_____
_____
_____
_____
_____
_____

Expansion Meditation

Begin by speaking the above invocation. Then, close your eyes and ground into your breath. Root your energy into the Earth and invite your higher self to support you in this meditation. As you breathe, feel the air flow in and out of your lungs, your body expands and contracts with each inhale and exhale. Feel into the flow of your life in its expansions and contractions. Consider the cycles of movement that are required to grow and deepen our wisdom. Connect with times you experienced contraction, felt squeezed, confused, or challenged in your life. Notice how it felt in your body. Remember times of expansion, when you took big leaps forward, your moments of success and realization of dreams, and times when miracles happened without effort.

See yourself moving into a time of great expansion. Feel possibilities and opportunities opening to you with ease and joy. If anything were possible, what would you want for your life? If you were assisted and supported every step of the way, what would you manifest? What would you create? What would you call in?

Imagine yourself experiencing this creation, this expansion. See the world around you as it would be if all your desires came true. Feel the excitement and gratitude of receiving these sacred desires. See yourself interacting with this world, moving through your days. Get as clear as you can in the details about how it feels, looks, and what you do. Welcome the experience into every cell of your body and allow this joy and excitement to light up with anticipation. Feel yourself saying "YES" to this vision with every fiber of your being.

Offer thanks to yourself, the Earth, and your higher self for helping you call forth this vision. Offer gratitude to the universe and spirit for bringing it into form.

Reflections on this meditation:

_____
_____
_____
_____
_____
_____
_____
_____
_____
_____

Card Spread

-1-
My deepest desire for my life is...

-2-
What does Spirit desire for me?

-3-
What can I release to create an opening to call in my desires?

-4-
What is being created through me?

Journal Prompts

Choose one or more of these questions each week to reflect and explore here or in your journal.

How do I define power in my life? How do I feel my power in my body?

How do I define freedom in my life? How do I feel freedom in my body?

In what areas of my life do I currently experience a sense of freedom and power?

If I could make the world just as I would like for it to be, what would it look/feel like? What would be different from how it is now?

If I could create absolutely anything I wanted, what would I create?

If my life were led by love, beauty, and joy, what would be different for me today? What would be different about my choices, thoughts, and feelings?

What do I perceive as blocks/obstacles to manifesting my highest vision for my life right now?

What changes do I need to make to be more aligned with my desires?

How can I commit to saying YES every day and step into my power? What would saying YES look like?

How can I commit to saying NO every day to that which does not serve me or my highest path? What would saying NO look like?

Monthly Rituals

Ritual Tea

- 1 part hawthorn leaf and flower
- 1/2 part damiana
- 1/2 part lavender
- ½ part orange peel
- ½ part cacao nibs
- ½ part real vanilla bean, chopped fine (1 inch for 32 oz tea)

Combine all herbs in a jar or teapot; pour boiling water over herbs and steep for 20 minutes. Strain.

Full Moon Ritual Bath

To a cup of Epsom or sea salt, add: a spoonful of honey, dried lavender, rose, and chamomile flowers, and jasmine and sandalwood essential oils (or any scents that make you feel extra sexy and powerful). As you stir it all together, call on the energy of your inner Queen. Feel yourself expanding and shining in your power. Send this energy into the salt mixture by focusing your attention on it. Add it to a warm bath.

Light some candles and put on some sultry music. Take some time in your luxurious bath to really connect with your body, touching every inch of yourself, starting with your feet, and working up. Love on your body in whatever way feels good to you. Let yourself feel like a goddess. When you're done, put on clothes that are comfortable and make you feel aligned with your inner Queen.

New Moon Candle Spell

Sprinkle a white candle with dried lavender flowers and anoint with your triple-rose oil. Gazing into the flame, summon your inner Lioness. Feel yourself embodying the energy of the Lioness, breathe her power and unapologetic fierceness into your heart space, sending it coursing through your veins.

Practice: Developing Intuition

Our bodies carry deep intelligence that our minds cannot easily access. Developing your inner knowing cultivates deeper trust in yourself. It makes tapping into your inner power easier by increasing the confidence in yourself. Intuition is known in Dialectical Behavioral Therapy as "Wise Mind"—considered the place where thoughts and feelings align to connect to a higher wisdom. Here is one way to work on enhancing your intuition.

First, do some reflection and writing on how you experience intuition now. How do you know it's speaking to you?

Now, do a grounding practice to connect yourself into the Earth. Breathe deeply and gently into your belly and bring your awareness to your body. Notice all the sensations in your body without trying to change them.

Practice saying NO in your mind while maintaining awareness of the experiences and sensations of your body. When you say NO, what does it feel like? For some, it can feel like a contraction or tightening, or a dropping in the belly. Your body is unique. Pay attention to how it communicates NO to you.

Write your observations here:

_____
_____
_____
_____

Once that feels complete, drop back into the breath, and bring awareness again to your body. Say YES in your mind while paying attention to the bodily sensations that arise. If it helps, think of something that feels good and is easy to say YES to. Some experience their YES as a softening, opening, and expanding in the chest or belly. Again, be present for how your body uniquely communicates YES.

Write your observations here:

_____
_____
_____
_____

Practice: Sex Magic and Queen Talisman

Sex magic is an incredibly potent form of manifestation. You may want to research sex magic as there is a lot to learn. When we orgasm, we are in a frequency of expansion, surrender, and pleasure. In this sex magic practice, we will harness our sexual energy into a talisman that represents pleasure and beauty. When you embody pleasure, joy, and power, it taps into your deepest, Spirit-led desires.

You will need:
- An object to be your talisman—piece of jewelry, like a ring or pendant
- A red or white candle
- A quiet space where you will not be disturbed

When you infuse your talisman with fire and sex magic, every time you wear it, you will embody feminine pleasure, beauty, and enhance your power to call more of it into your life. Choose a stone that aligns with feminine magic, such as moonstone, labradorite, or rose quartz, or sun magic such as carnelian or citrine. Choose a piece of jewelry you already have, or buy a special piece to honor your sex magic. Whatever you choose, cleanse it with smoke, fresh salt water, or in the moonlight. *Note: Water can damage some stones. Do not cleanse: turquoise, black tourmaline, pyrite, hematite, lapis lazuli, moonstone, opal, or selenite with water.*

During your journaling time this month, write a statement claiming your desire, pleasure, joy, and power. It can be as simple as: *"I claim and embody my desire, pleasure, joy, and power. I create the world I want to live in."* It can be an affirmation from this chapter or a statement that aligns with you.

Take the ritual bath (see Page 111). Make the bath sensual and beautiful with a playlist that evokes feelings of pleasure and sexuality. Speak your statement out loud several times in the bath. Afterward, anoint yourself with your Triple Rose Oil or a fragrance that makes you feel beautiful and powerful. Put on sexy clothes (or nothing at all!) and get in bed or wherever you can be alone and undisturbed, and you feel comfortable and safe.

Light a red or white candle, and put on music. Hold your chosen talisman in your right hand and gaze into your candle. Bring the energy of the flame into your root and womb space. Lay down in bed and feel the warmth of the flame of desire in your body. If you use both hands to bring yourself to orgasm, place your talisman on your lower belly and send energy into it. Take your time—at least 15 to 20 minutes. Touch yourself the way you like to be touched. Explore, enjoy, and bring yourself to orgasm. Build the energy by coming close to climax and come down several times before you climax. When you feel the waves of orgasm washing over you, speak your affirmation (*in your head or out loud*). Send the energy of your orgasm into the jewelry and feel it become infused and filled with your power and the power of fire.

When you are done, send gratitude to Earth, Spirit, and your body for its incredible power of creation. Wear your talisman anytime you want to call on the energy of your inner fire and personal power.

Celebrate Summer Solstice!

June 20th–22nd in the Northern Hemisphere
December 20th–22nd in the Southern Hemisphere

Summer Solstice is the longest day of the year, both a celebration of the long days of hard work toward the inevitable harvest and a releasing of the light as the days begin to shorten toward winter.

It is the midpoint of our year, a time to reflect on all that you have worked on so far: surrender and connection to Spirit, healing and forgiveness, cultivating relationships with your Inner Child and Inner Maiden, deepening your self-awareness, self-love, discernment, and inner authority. Through all of this, you get clearer on what you want for yourself. As we step into the Queen energy of June, you will claim your sovereignty, your right to be in this world unapologetically, and get more comfortable in the everyday embodiment of your unique power and brilliance.

During the fiery time of Summer Solstice, I like to honor the Goddess Lilith. Her story (rooted in Jewish mythology) tells of a woman who was created as Adam's equal in the Garden of Eden. She refused to be subjugated by him. Instead, she chose to walk out of the Garden and make a life for herself. She is a potent role-model for standing in your truth and authority. Lilith shows us how to write our stories instead of allowing ourselves to be defined by other's perceptions. Lilith is a very powerful goddess. I recommend learning more about her, honoring her with offerings, and cultivating a relationship with her before attempting to do any spell work or magic with her assistance. This is true for all the goddesses mentioned in this book, but especially for Lilith!

Offerings for Lilith: Red roses, wine, dance, poetry, sex, candles, dragon's blood incense

Since Summer celebrates the element of Fire, the heat of desire and passion, the flames of transformation, the power of our will, and the joy of creativity stirring in our bellies, here are some recommendations for working with this element.

Season: Summer
Element: Fire
Tarot : Suit of Wands
Direction: South
Time of day: High noon
Symbology: Action, will, passion, transformation, and creativity
Body: Solar Plexus
Magical tools: Hearth fires, bonfires, candles, cooking, sun energy

Fire magic is great for release and transformation, as well as increasing power and energy around any actions you are taking. What is your relationship with Fire? I often think of camping trips and sitting around a campfire in circle with my community. Fire brings people together. It's elusive, dangerous, and powerful. Meditate on areas you'd like a little more Fire in your life and welcome its energies into those places.

Think about what sparks and feeds your inner flame. Connect with the element of Fire by welcoming the energy of the sun into your body and feeling it fill you with warmth and passion. Tap into your sensual nature and explore ways to give yourself pleasure. Play! Have a little campfire in your backyard or light a candle daily to stoke the flames of your dreams.

Candle magic is a potent and simple way to work with the element of Fire. Candles hold the energy of your intentions and can be chosen by color to embody certain energies. You can infuse candles with your intentions, anoint them with oils and herbs, carve sigils and words into them, and work with them to establish sacred space. I also light candles to hold energy for simple intentions, such as supporting a friend who is sick or struggling, giving strength or confidence if I have an important meeting or event happening, or holding an intention of love and peace in a space.

Create a Sigil Candle Spell

This spell combines the focused intention of a sigil with the amplifying and energizing effect of candle magic. Your previous spells and personal reflections will support you in creating the most concentrated, powerful spell to harness the fertile energy of summer to manifest what you want. Think about your surrendering work and what you identified is within your power. Your healing and unbinding work will help you create an intention from a place of wholeness, sovereignty, and clarity. Use your vision board to inspire what is possible for you now. Review your values and align the possibilities with your sense of purpose and who you want to be. Think big, envision your desires for 5, 10, and 20 years from now. See yourself *exactly* where you want to be. Be mindful and open to guidance from Spirit, because often what we think is best for us is limiting. *This is a powerful spell to do with a group, too.*

You will need:
- A beeswax candle (we use bee medicine for its powers of industriousness, cooperation, healing, intelligence, and service)
- A nail or knife for carving
- Fire and heat-proof bowl
- Triple Rose Oil or other anointing oil
- Recommended herbs (choose what speaks to you depending on your intention and use anything else from your personal practice and local environment):
  - Juniper or Cedar—Divine support and protection
  - Roses—unconditional love, high vibration, heart healing
  - Motherwort—nurturing

- Calendula—beauty, soothing, sun energy
- Nettle—discernment, strength, protection
- Lavender—healing, calming, balance, beauty
- Yarrow—balancing, boundaries, courage
- Damiana—feminine power and desire, sexuality, magic
- Cinnamon—abundance, warmth, richness of life
- Rosemary—clarity, cleansing, focus
- Mullein—softening, soothing grief, lung healing
- Mugwort—visions, dreams, protection

Begin by casting a circle with your wand or sacred salt. Call the directions, root yourself into the Earth, and invoke your guides, angels, well ancestors, and higher self. Meditate and write out your intentions. Create your sigil according to the directions on Page 95. Carve your sigil into your candle. Add other symbols, images, or words that support the energy of your intention. Once your candle is carved, anoint it all over with your oil of choice. Combine your chosen herbs and grind them into a powder with a mortar and pestle. Rub them onto your candle and take care to get the herbs into all the carvings on your candle. Place the candle in a holder and also in a fireproof bowl.

IMPORTANT: See fire safety tips on Page 27.

Light the candle on the Solstice and let it burn down all the way. Close your circle and offer gratitude to all of your helpers.

Monthly Reflections

What was most challenging for me this month?
_____
_____
_____

What was most rewarding? What growth have I witnessed in myself?
_____
_____
_____

Magical associations to the Queen:
_____
_____
_____

Tree, herb, flower, and plant allies I worked with:
_____
_____
_____

Animal allies I worked with:
_____
_____
_____

Stone allies I worked with:

Songs:

Scents:

Food and drink:

People, Deities, Role Models:

My Personal Practices: *What am I learning about my personal magic through these practices?*

Queen

When I am very still inside, I begin to feel the shape of my future. It asks something of me. I must get very quiet to hear the question.

I leave behind the old ways, let go of worry, and read minds. Ease of guilt and rooting into joy, I feel an unfolding of my home like roses unfolding from their buds. My child growing inside me, being born and long days nursing, watching the hawks hunting from my back porch. The hum of the road under me, the vision of lazy summer days in places I've never seen before. The constant return to what is true for me: family, home, writing, love, connection. The remembering in my bones of sovereignty and stillness, sacred waters softening my skin, sisterhood and laughter and living big and loud, no apologies.

Steaming pots of broth bubble through quiet mornings. Rowdy Sunday picnics and mud tracks through my kitchen bring smiles. Lavender blooming, rabbits munching on tender greens in the garden, shooing them away with a broom only for them to return. The scent of sacred incense infused in the very walls and hints of magic in every doorway and corner.

My peaceful feelings help others keep a fierce loyalty to my boundaries. I allow myself to lead and rest. I read in bed with my children and teach them the ways of magic. I am present here, as I age, as I deepen into myself. I do not miss the past. I do not regret. I do not compare.

I watch the moon rise and pull her down into me. I gather with my sisters around the fire and hold space for one another in our tears, anger, softness, and bliss. I grow things and make things and weave things and burn things. I watch the sun set over snowy mountains. I feel sexier than ever before.

I take my partner's hand in mine and feel the warmth of years and years of good night kisses and long talks over whiskey on ice and decorating Christmas trees and sharing furtive glances of pride when our children show kindness to others. It spreads in my hand and travels to my heart, and back through to my lover's heart.

The strength in my body and breath of the land, the protection of the knotty junipers surrounding our home, the soft hoot of a great horned owl and wild cackles of the coyotes, the gentle creak and sway of a porch swing. I am grateful. I am great. I am full.

CHAPTER SEVEN
JULY

"I am a warrior. My boundaries are sacred."

JULY IS THE HEART of summer, wildfires, transformation, passion, heat, and wild play. As harvest time comes closer, we discern with whom we are sharing our harvest, and wanting to be in community as we prepare for colder months and darker days. We are invited into relationship and clarity with our boundaries when they are being violated and how to stand in our integrity when they are not respected. We stand strong and fight for what matters to us. We are no longer dominated by others. We trust our power and speak our truth, and trust others enough to either accept our boundaries or leave.

PROTECTION ✦ BOUNDARIES ✦ STRENGTH ✦ JUSTICE

THE WOLF/WARRIOR

The Warrior is our protector. Our Inner Warrior comes out when our "fight, flight, freeze, or fawn" response activates. These responses are created to protect our inner child. However, if the Warrior has not been trained and disciplined to serve, The Warrior can be reactive and explosive, or overly fearful and self-defensive. We are all worthy of and in need of an inner protector, one who tells us when we are in danger, stands up to those who would harm us, and fights for justice and liberation. When our boundaries are clear and sacred, we can let go of reactivity and fear, and put our Warrior to work when it is truly appropriate.

THE WOUND: Fear/lack of safety

THE HEALING: Boundaries

ELEMENT: Fire

PLANT ALLY: Yarrow

Yarrow is commonly used in boundary and protection work. It is also good for healing wounds and calming inflammation (when we feel too "fired up"). It gives us courage in times of fear.

ANIMAL ALLY: Wolf

The Wolf has a tragic history in the United States but is now making a triumphant comeback in many places out west. When wolves are allowed to live in harmony with their environment, the rest of the environment comes into balance as well. This teaches us that even though wolves are fiercely protective of their territory and pack, their power in strength, courage, and boundaries are what keep the rest of the ecosystem in balance.

STONE ALLY: Obsidian

Work with this stone to clear obstacles and remove toxicity from your life, or work with it as an ally for protection and fierce boundaries. This stone's volcanic origins give it a sharp edge, if needed, and the fire within can burn if your boundaries are not respected.

Monthly Themes

Protection is a concept that we need to invoke every day. Protection not only from those who may harm us, but protection from our negative thoughts, feelings, and beliefs that keep us from living in our truth. As grown adults, we must protect ourselves from those who have their own interest at heart and not ours. Negativity, doubt, and internal systems of control are powerful forces that interfere with our connection to the Divine and our ability to manifest our highest path. Take ownership of your protection so you are no longer a victim to systems that do not consider your best interests.

Boundaries are the next step in our spiritual and magical evolution. Having boundaries is a fierce act of self-love. We are discouraged from setting our boundaries, which can cause us to be used and exploited. We are only responsible for our boundaries, not how others interpret or respond to them. If they activate others' wounding and fear, that is their work to do. If we neglect our boundaries for fear of how they will be received, we communicate to those around us that they should do that, too. Boundaries communicate that we have a right to say *No* to that which is not in service to us. We have a right to say *No* to that which would harm us. Saying *No* is not harmful to others. Seeking to manipulate others by compromising our own boundaries is harmful. Not honoring our boundaries in relationships leads to resentment and a whole host of other toxic patterns that are harmful to ourselves and the people we are in relationship with. This month, commit to clarifying and honoring your boundaries and be in right relationship to yourself, others, and the Earth.

Strength is what springs from us when we are protected and have clear and loving boundaries. Our energy is not being sucked by unloving relationships and situations, and we are no longer ruminating in fear and self-limitation. We know where we end and begin, what is acceptable to us, and what is not. We make choices from those places with confidence. Strength is having a full cup because we put ourselves first. Strength is showing up for others in integrity because we do not feel obligated to sacrifice ourselves for them.

Justice is clarity of right and wrong as we are guided on our spiritual path. It is holding systems and people (including ourselves) accountable for the harm we cause others and making true amends. Our culture values justice only as it serves those in power and compromises justice if it threatens the power and control of the dominant forces in our society. This causes us to be out of balance, and what we create from imbalance is out of balance as well. We cannot be in integrity without justice, period. Expansive, loving, collaborative, healing ways of being are not accessible without justice, period. Begin by cultivating justice in yourself. Align your actions with your values, personal truths, and deep inner knowing. Be kind and compassionate with yourself while maintaining integrity to your highest path. Ask yourself before any action, *"Is this the most loving, honest, aligned action I can take for myself and others?"*

Affirmations

I am strong and protected.

I stand in my truth.

I honor my boundaries.

I respect my integrity and seek justice in all things.

My personal affirmations:

_____
_____
_____
_____

Daily Invocation

Spirit, today I call on your protection. Protect me from harm, fear, and manipulation. Help me see clearly where I am not honored, loved, and respected. May I stand in my truth and claim my right to be honored, loved, and respected. Today, I love, honor, and respect myself. I meet the challenges of my day with strength. I release all attachment to pleasing others at the expense of my well-being. Help me see when this is happening so I can change my actions to be in alignment with my highest path. Blessed be.

My personal intentions and prayers:

_____
_____
_____
_____
_____
_____
_____
_____

Energy Hygiene and Protection Meditation

Ground your energy into the Earth through your breath. Feel your energy rooting and anchoring you to the Earth. Call up all the energy in your body that doesn't belong to you, that you are holding in your body and your energetic field, and send it down your roots into the Earth. Any energy that no longer serves you and is ready to be released can also be sent down these roots into the Earth.

Now, call your energy back to you, all the energy you have left with others, or in memories or unrealized desires. Feel it coming back into your body. Welcome it with open arms. Clear your energy by inviting the breath into all the cells of your body, clearing and cleansing your energetic field.

Breathe into your heart space. Feel the love from your heart beginning to grow and extend outward. See your energy as a bubble of light. Watch it grow and surround you, like a cell membrane. You can see through it but nothing is allowed into your energetic field without your explicit permission. Choose a color for your energetic field that feels protective to you (red and spiky can feel protective in conflict, blue can feel like spiritual and psychic protection, green can feel healing and soothing). Imagine yourself moving through the world with this protective barrier that allows you to decide what comes into your energy field and what doesn't.

Do this visualization regularly, so you can energetically feel the difference when you activate your protective cell membrane. Continue to practice visualization until it happens naturally, and you consistently feel protected, grounded, and clear in your energetic field.

Reflections on this meditation:

_____
_____
_____
_____
_____
_____
_____
_____
_____
_____
_____
_____

Card Spread

-1-
What does my Inner Warrior want me to know right now?

_____
_____
_____
_____
_____

-2-
What gets in the way of accessing my Inner Warrior?

_____
_____
_____
_____
_____

-3-
Where do I need to strengthen my boundaries?

_____
_____
_____
_____
_____

-4-
Where is justice being called for in my life today?

_____
_____
_____
_____
_____

Journal Prompts

Choose one or more of these questions each week to reflect and explore here or in your journal.

In what ways am I protected in my life today? In what ways am I needing protection?

What is my relationship to boundaries right now? Where do I struggle with holding my boundaries? Where do I need to be accountable for allowing my boundaries to be violated by not standing up for myself?

How can I be more aligned to honor my boundaries today?

When I reflect on my relationship to fear, what thoughts, feelings, and sensations arise?

What helps calm my fear to help me stand more firmly in my truth?

How have I been betrayed by others? How have I betrayed myself? How have I betrayed others?

What would justice look like for me? What does justice feel like in my body?

I call on protection for:

I claim these boundaries for myself:

I call on strength for:

Monthly Rituals

Ritual Tea

1 part yarrow
1 part peppermint
1 part elderflower

Combine all herbs in a jar or teapot; pour boiling water over herbs and steep for 20 minutes. Strain.

Full Moon Ritual Bath

In a warm bath, sprinkle a handful of fresh or dried yarrow flowers, a cup of Epsom or sea salt, plus a few drops of rosemary and patchouli essential oils, and light candles all around your bath. While soaking, connect with the medicine of the wolf. Breathe into your heart space and feel where you need boundaries and strength. Feel the wolf energy growing in your heart to protect and guide you in your boundaries. See that energy activating in the water around you and in the cells of your body. Feel the energy amplified by the power of the full moon. If desired, when your bath is complete, step out of the tub and go outside to stand naked under the full moon. Give it a howl and bring the beautiful energy of the moon down into your heart space by raising your hands to the moon and pulling them down to your heart.

New Moon Candle Spell

Anoint a black candle with Triple Rose oil and roll in or sprinkle with dried or fresh yarrow flower. Write the following on a piece of paper:

What I am saying NO to:

What I am saying YES to:

I call on strength for:

Light your altar candle. Speak what you wrote into the flames. Then burn the paper in the fire. *Use a fire-proof bowl to catch the ashes—you can use these ashes for your Black Salt (see Page 129).* Allow the candle to burn down all the way.

Practice: Black Protection Salt

Witch's Black Salt is a common spell to use for protection and boundaries. Work with it to create protection in a circle for ceremony or spell work, sprinkled over thresholds, in corners of rooms, around your property, or carried with you in a purse or knapsack while traveling. Here is the basic recipe for Black Salt:

- Sea Salt
- Finely ground Charcoal (you can save charcoal from sacred ceremonial fires for this if you like)
- Black pepper
- Dried rosemary

1. Combine your ingredients and call on Spirit for protection and sacred boundaries as you blend.
2. Store the mixed salt in a jar with a lid.

My personal variation on this Salt is Ancestor Black Salt, to infuse with the support and protection of our ancestors. To make Ancestor Black Salt, follow the directions below.

1. With a mortar and pestle, combine the following:
    - Sea Salt – clearing and purification, holds intentions, protective, absorbs and clears negative energy
    - Charcoal – protective and absorbs energy
    - Rosemary – purification, protection, clarity
    - Mugwort – witch's ally, protection, divination and vision, connection to spirit realms
    - Elderflower – ancestral protection, good health, calming, and supportive
    - Yarrow – protection from negativity, balance, courage, healing
    - Patchouli – breaks hexes, repels negativity, and enhances power
    - Desert sage – purity, protection, cleansing, clearing, wisdom, and vision
    - Juniper berries – protection from evil, purifying, healing, connection to spirit realms and nature
    - Black pepper – repellent, banish negative energy, protective

2. Seal in a jar holding your intentions for the salt in your mind. If desired, put your hand over the jar and speak the following: *"I call on the power of my ancestors in the spirit realm who are here for my highest good to protect me (or this space) from harm and negativity, to cleanse me and purify me, to provide safety, clarity, and vision, and to support me in all my endeavors. Blessed be!"*

*Please note that Black Salt can stain furniture, carpet, and windowsills. Salt placed by your home for protection should not be placed near plants. The salt can harm your plants.

Practice: Protection Herb Bundles

- Hang by the door of your home for protection.
- Burn to clear the energy of your home with sacred smoke, and ask spirit for protection.
- Use your herb bundle to brush over your body. You can also sprinkle yourself with salt water for extra cleansing and to clear negative energy and fear.

Ask permission from your plant allies, if you can take a fresh sprig from each of the following:
- Rosemary – purification, protection
- Sage – cleansing, purifying, protective, strengthening
- Juniper – purification, cleansing, healing
- Lavender – protection, love, calming, healing, clarity
- Cedar – purification, cleansing, protection of spirit guides
- Roses – love, healing, high vibration, connection to Divine, good luck

Use hemp twine to bind the herb sprigs together in a tight bundle. Decorate your bundle by wrapping the bottom with a piece of leather cord as a hand hold, or add beads, stones, feathers, or whatever you like. For burning, allow your bundle to dry thoroughly, about 2-4 weeks.

Prepare for the Next Celebration!

Lughnasa (also spelled Lughnasadh), or Lammas, is celebrated on August 1st in the Northern Hemisphere and February 1st in the Southern Hemisphere. In Gaelic traditions, it is the first harvest festival of the season.

Items to prepare or have on hand for your altar:

Fresh berries

Fresh baked bread with rosemary and salt

Corn, fresh herbs, anything you are harvesting from your own garden

Red, orange, and yellow candles

Items that represent sun energy: sunflowers, yellow and gold clothing, fire

Coins, honey, acorns, cinnamon, and anything that represents an abundant harvest

Monthly Reflections

What was most challenging for me this month?

___

___

___

What was most rewarding? What growth have I witnessed in myself?

___

___

___

Magical associations to the Warrior:

___

___

___

Tree, herb, flower, and plant allies I worked with:

___

___

___

Animal allies I worked with:

___

___

___

Stone allies I worked with:

_____
_____
_____

Songs:

_____
_____
_____

Scents:

_____
_____

Food and drink:

_____
_____
_____

People, Deities, Role Models:

_____
_____
_____

My Personal Practices: *What am I learning about my personal magic through these practices?*

_____
_____
_____
_____

Self-Love is a Boundary

As we become liberated through our work, it is our responsibility to support and actively engage in the liberation of all people. This is integrity and congruence. We can learn to truly love ourselves, be gentle and kind with our bodies, listen to our needs and make space for them, and deconstruct the patriarchy within us that says: "hustle, succeed, achieve, never slow down or show weakness, have it all, be perfect, be thin, be desirable, be pleasant, be quiet." Then, we can translate to our systems and institutions a softer, more loving, and open way of being in the world. We begin to understand there is no other choice. We cannot fully embody unconditional self-love while being complicit in an unloving system.

CHAPTER EIGHT
AUGUST

"I create life, beauty, and art. I am my most Divine creation."

AUGUST IS THE doorway to the harvest season—a time to take stock of what we are reaping from our energetic labors and deciding what we want to make of it—a time to make bread of wheat, wreaths of dried flowers, jam from fresh berries. What do you want to make from all you have learned, all you have called in? This month you are invited to delight in your inspiration and creativity, and honor your unique gifts.

Inspiration ✦ Passion ✦ Creativity ✦ Uniqueness

The Artist

The Artist lives within us all. She is filled with passion and inspiration for all she does and expresses her unique voice through the medium that calls most deeply to her in the moment— painting, writing, cooking, tending her garden, raising children, or anything else. If we allow ourselves to be guided by the Artist within, all actions will be creative and generative.

The Wound: Self-silencing/conformity

The Healing: Creativity

Element: Fire

Plant Ally: Damiana
Commonly known as an aphrodisiac, Damiana ignites feminine passion and creativity. This plant ally assists in tuning into and activating our desires.

Animal Ally: Snake
Snakes represent the creative life force within us. As Snake sheds its skin, it is constantly revealing new versions of itself. Through constant transformation and renewal, the Snake helps us remember that our lives and how we move through the world are our greatest works of art.

Stone Ally: Citrine
A beautiful ally for life force, creativity, prosperity, flow, and inspiration, Citrine can be worked with any time you want to help intentions or creations grow generously and beautifully.

Monthly Themes

Inspiration: What inspires you? What lights you up, excites you, pleases you, and encourages you? When we don't take time to cultivate inspiration, life can feel dull and monotonous. We have been living in intense and challenging times. To get us through darkness, we must believe something more beautiful is coming. We cannot create a beautiful future without connecting to what inspires us now, for that inspiration is the foundation of weaving a magical, powerful vision for what's next.

Passion: The pleasure of creativity comes from the force of our passion. It gives us drive, focus, and power behind our creations. Passion is Divinely guided and shows us that doing the work doesn't always have to feel like work. Sometimes work is more like play, or being "in the flow" of our true life's purpose.

Creativity: When we allow ourselves to be inspired by others and allow passion to flow freely, the brilliance of others and ourselves integrates—this is how creativity builds upon itself. The creative force lives inside us. When creativity is suppressed, we feel dissatisfied with life. We were made to create, and this is the meaning of "God made us in their image." In fact, we are infinitely powerful creators, as you are hopefully experiencing through cultivating a deeper spiritual and magical life. When we cultivate a spiritual life, everything around us changes. Our energy, thoughts, and reactions create our experiences, relationships, and environments. It's time to create something truly wonderful! Create magic by honoring the creative force in you, in whatever form it wishes to take.

Uniqueness: While our dominant culture values conformity for the perpetuation of the status quo, you were meant to shine in your unique brilliance. Mother Nature loves diversity—to her it means collaboration, survival, resilience, and connection. Without it, the world dies. Even if your gifts feel small and insignificant, they are not! Whatever you bring to the table is needed. Your special brilliance is a welcome contribution and new perspective in building a more loving way of life.

Affirmations

I am a work of art.

My brilliance is a gift to the world.

Passion and inspiration flow freely through me.

I inspire others with my unique gifts.

My personal affirmations:

_____
_____
_____
_____

Daily Invocation

Spirit, today, I call on Divine inspiration in all my actions. Show me the pleasure of passion and the joy of creating for creation's sake. Help me trust my contributions and unique brilliance. Make my life a work of art, in service to creating a beautiful tapestry of life, and honoring the diversity of the Earth as our guide.

My personal intentions and prayers:

_____
_____
_____
_____
_____
_____
_____
_____

Snake Meditation

Begin by grounding with your breath. Bring awareness to all the cells of your body. Feel your body relax as you breathe. Root your energy into the Earth. Breathe your roots deeper and deeper into the Earth, until you reach the liquid fire core of the planet. Feel the heat, movement, and power of the creative force deep within the Earth as a spinning, swirling ball of fiery metal. Bring this energy up through your roots, inviting a smaller version of this ball of energy into your root where your body meets the seat of your chair. See it spinning and glowing, Feel the ball warm your blood and light up all your cells. Imagine your body as a sacred cave. This ball of light is the fire warming and illuminating the cavern. On the walls of the cavern are beautiful paintings—images of things and experiences that you created. See yourself sitting by the fire, feel the sense of inspiration and empowerment these images create. Gaze into the fire. See a red snake undulating in the flames, shedding its skin to reveal more of itself to you. As you look at the snake, your energies align. Now, you are the snake in the fire. Feel the fire shedding your old skin, revealing a Divine creator ready to be seen, filled with passion and vision of what you are creating. See the images on the wall of your cave as you dream them. Watch as they project into your life and allow yourself to feel excitement in the unfolding of these creations. Feel yourself experiencing what you've created and the joy of embodying your creative power.

Pull these images and sensations into your womb space and allow them to settle into your cells, blood, organs and bone. Know you can return to this sacred cave at any time, when you wish to activate the energy of raw creation. Offer thanks to the Earth, the snake, and this sacred cave of creativity and transformation. Offer thanks to your miraculous body and your brilliant imagination and desires.

When you feel ready, you may leave the cave and return your awareness to your physical body and the room you are in. Take your time opening your eyes and coming back to the present moment.

Reflections on this meditation:

Card Spread

-1-
How do I get in the way of expressing my creativity?

-2-
What assists me to be in my creative flow?

-3-
What does Spirit wish to co-create through me?

-4-
What am I creating right now?

Journal Prompts:

Choose one or more of these questions each week to reflect and explore here or in your journal.

What is my relationship to creativity?

What thoughts, feelings, and sensations arise when I reflect on my creativity?

Where have I felt blocked creatively?

How do I experience passion and inspiration in my body?

How do I honor or suppress these feelings?

What/who inspires me?

How can I incorporate more sources of inspiration in my life now?

When have I felt most creative and inspired in my life? How can I cultivate this every day?

What do I wish to create?

What am I not creating that I want to? Why?

What unique perspectives do I bring to my life and community?

What is my relationship to what makes me unique? Do I honor and celebrate this, or seek to hide it?

Monthly Rituals

Ritual Tea

- 1 part damiana
- 1 part hibiscus
- 1 part lemon verbena
- Optional: ¼ part licorice for sweetness

Combine all herbs in a glass jar. Fill with cold water and set out in the sunshine to steep all day. Strain and serve over ice.

Full Moon Ritual Bath

Blend a cup of Epsom or sea salt with damiana, hibiscus, sunflower petals, and a few drops of ylang-ylang essential oil (the hibiscus will turn the water pink). As you run your bath, add the salt blend and stir gently with your hand. Listen to or recite the snake meditation on Page 138 and imagine the energy of the snake in the flames filling the water. Ask for Divine inspiration, passion, and creativity to infuse the water and all the cells of your body.

New Moon Candle Spell

Anoint a red candle with the Triple Rose Oil (Page 44). Sprinkle or roll the candle in damiana herb. Light the candle, and ask for the spirit of damiana to fill you with passion and inspiration to create your life as a unique work of art. Gaze into the flame and allow any images to come to you. Afterward, take time to journal about your experience with the candle meditation and feel deeply into your body. Reflect on what it is like to be filled with a passionate fire for life.

Practice: Creativity Spell Bag

Spell/Charm bags have many uses and come in many different forms. This one is designed to call on the brilliant parts of you, including your Higher Self, Inner Child, Maiden, and Queen to integrate into the whole of what makes you unique and allows you to stand fully in your creative power. This spell is very basic and can be adapted to your personal skill set and what you have on hand.

You will need:

- A square of cloth (if possible, choose something that has personal significance to you, like a handkerchief from your favorite aunt, or a pattern with your favorite flower on it. If you are not the sewing type, you can also use a pre-made pouch with a drawstring or zipper)
- Needle and thread
- Any other type of decoration you like patches, beads, and feathers.
- Items (plants, stones, charms, etc) that call on the energy of these parts of you. Try these:
  - Higher Self: juniper berries or clear quartz
  - Spirit/the Divine: rose petals
  - Wild child: dandelion flowers or seeds (or any type of flower/herb she likes)
  - Maiden: calendula flowers or amethyst
  - Queen: lavender flowers, anything gold, or a few drops of jasmine oil
  - Carnelian for creativity and inspiration
  - Acorns to represent infinite potential
  - Snakeskin for transformation and creative life force
  - Anything that represents your unique creativity (for instance, if you are a chef, put in a copy of your favorite recipe; if you are a writer, put in a nub of a pencil)

This is your personal spell bag, so make it your own! Put in things that inspire you, that light you up, that fill you with energy to create! I have listed nine different elements to include because that is a powerful number for me in my magic. Choose a number that has personal significance for you.

To construct your Spell Bag, fold your fabric in half with the fabric inside out. Sew three of the four sides together, to make a pouch. Turn it right side out. If you wish, sew a symbol on the front to represent creativity, or add patches, beads, or any kind of decoration that pleases you. Make it fun, and don't be too serious! Add your magical elements to the bag. Fasten the fourth side closed with a drawstring, button, or safety pin. It's okay to leave the bag open so you can look inside and connect with the contents or add new things.

Keep your Spell Bag on your altar, hang it from your bedpost, or make a necklace and wear it whenever you wish to activate your creativity.

Items in my Spell Bag and what they represent for me:

_____
_____
_____
_____
_____
_____
_____
_____
_____
_____

Practice: Create an Inspiring Playlist

Music is medicine and has a direct impact on our energy and neuropathways. Think about the music you like. Does it inspire you, lift you up, and help you imagine the best version of yourself? Or does it sometimes keep you stuck in negative thinking or emotions? There's nothing wrong with putting on some sad music to have a good cry, or something that helps you work through rage or betrayal. But I encourage you to be mindful about how you use music to affect your energetic state and frame of mind. Music can be a powerful tool to help you create yourself as the brilliant work of art that you are!

This month, make a playlist of music that inspires you to create, sparks your passions, and celebrates your uniqueness. Here are some songs/artists I follow who do that for me:

Beyonce (obviously): *Black Parade, Formation, Run the World, Spirit*
King Princess: *Holy*
Banks: *Goddess*
Lizzy Jeff: *Drip, Goddess Code*
Michael Franti: *The Flower, Little Things*
Ayla Nereo: *Show Yourself*
Andra Day: *Rise Up*
Rising Appalachia: *Speak Out, Spirit's Cradle, Medicine*
The Chicks: *March March*
Linda Diaz: *Green Tea Ice Cream*
India Arie: *Beautiful, I am Light, I Am (with Beautiful Chorus), Video*

The Wailin' Jennys: *Light of a Clear Blue Morning, Wildflowers*
Beautiful Chorus: *My Little Light, Inner Peace, Fierce Grace*
Heather Maloney: *Dandelion*
Shylah Ray Sunshine: *Into the Wild*
Sade: *Flower of the Universe*
Mary Isis: *She is Boundless, Good Things Take Time*
Lizzo: *Good as Hell*
Snatam Kaur: *Ra Ma Da Sa, Servant of Peace*
Lila: *Ancestors*
Joy Williams: *Woman (Oh Mama), All I Need*
Deya Dova: *Myth of the Cave*
Cold War Kids: *Complainer*
MaMuse: *Natural Order*
Alexia Chellun: *As I Wake in the Morning, Abundance, The River*

My favorite inspiring songs:

Celebrate Lughnasa!

August 1st in the Northern Hemisphere
February 1st in the Southern Hemisphere

August, September, and October are months of harvest, a time to celebrate the bounty of our hard work over the summer and a preparation time for the cold, dark winter months ahead. Traditionally Lughnasa is the first harvest festival of this season. During this festival, Demeter is the perfect Goddess to honor. In Greek mythology, Demeter represents the bounty of the harvest and the Divine Mother energy of abundance, fertility, nurturing, and providing for the community. As an offering to Demeter, you can place on your altar: bread, honey, acorns, and cinnamon sticks.

Celebrate Lughnasa by gathering your best friends and making Golden Harvest Abundance Honey. This spell is an embodiment of creativity, productivity, fertility, abundance, celebration, and community.

Golden Harvest Abundance Honey

Work with to this honey to call in and embody the sweetness of abundance and prosperity every day! In a small mason jar, add the following:

- Cinnamon sticks – attraction, spice and fire, desire, abundance
- Cloves – attracts wealth and prosperity, love, and passion
- Bee Pollen – industriousness and productivity, attraction, love, happiness, abundance
- Star Anise – expansion, connection to Divine, success, and luck
- Ginger root – fiery and energetic, adds power and heat, speeds things up
- Calendula – optimism, vitality, attracts success, dispels negativity
- Cacao nibs – heart opener, connection to higher self, embodiment, balance of masculine and feminine energy, creativity, and joy
- Chamomile – healing, soothing, calming, prosperous, attraction, and luck
- Citrine – confidence, efficacy, prosperity, abundance, trust in one's inner authority

Pour raw local honey over the above list of ingredients. Ring bells, dance, pull cards, and celebrate over your Golden Harvest Abundance Honey, infusing it with your energy of celebration, joy, and the sweetness of life! Infuse for 2-4 weeks. Strain and stir into tea or eat by the spoonful.

Prepare for the Next Celebration!

Autumn Equinox, or Mabon, falls between September 21st and 23rd in the Northern Hemisphere and March 21st and 22nd in the Southern Hemisphere, marking the balance between night and day and the lengthening nights toward the Winter Solstice.

Some items to prepare, have on hand, and/or put on your altar:

Fresh bread, corn, wheat, pumpkins and other squash, apples, nuts, mushrooms

Rowan berries

Cinnamon, anise, clove, and allspice

Cauldron or chalice filled with water, charged under a full moon or with your blessings and intentions whispered into it

Orange, red, gold, and brown candles

Autumn foliage to decorate your home

Collect fallen branches for your Pentacle (see Page 160)

Monthly Reflections

What was most challenging for me this month?
_____
_____
_____

What was most rewarding? What growth have I witnessed in myself?
_____
_____
_____

Magical associations to the Artist:
_____
_____
_____

Tree, herb, flower, and plant allies I worked with:
_____
_____
_____

Animal allies I worked with:
_____
_____
_____

Stone allies I worked with:

_____
_____
_____

Songs:

_____
_____

Scents:

_____
_____

Food and drink:

_____
_____
_____

People, Deities, Role Models:

_____
_____
_____

My Personal Practices: *What am I learning about my personal magic through these practices?*

_____
_____
_____
_____

The Timing is Now

Last night I dreamed of a massive river flowing down a massive mountain. I rode the tumbles and rapids of the river. In my dream, I knew this water well, like an old friend. The water was clear blue, deep, and moving swiftly.

I came upon a fork in this mighty river. To the left, the river moved gracefully down the mountain with stairs under the water, offering safe passage to those traveling with the current. To the right, the water soared over a cliff, tumbling into an even greater body of water hundreds of feet below. The turquoise beauty of it called to me like a siren, urging me to jump.

I knew in my dream that I had made this jump before. My heart pounded, contemplating it with excitement and also deep fear of the unknown…would I survive the fall? Would I enjoy the excitement?

I wasn't ready. There was a cabin perched atop the river built to overlook the waterfall and harness the potent energy of the moving water. There was a small bed and table inside, and I made myself a little home there. A friend visited. I'm not sure why she was there…perhaps we were both preparing to jump.

Now, I am perched atop a waterfall preparing for a jump I know I've done before. I know there is the option to take the "safer" route. I know either choice is okay—there is no wrong way to go in nature. All is learning, all is growth. I also know I love the exhilaration of the jump, and rush as I choose to radically trust in myself and in the Earth, radical trust in each step (or leap) she guides me toward.

Here we are, our options and distractions and to-do lists ripped away from us, challenging us to live fully in this present moment and tend to our bodies, hearts, and loved one, which forces us to surrender to the unknown. And so I ask myself: what is known to me? What desires and dreams live in my body that have been patiently (or not so patiently) waiting for me to leap into with radical trust, waiting behind a barrage of reasons why "the timing isn't right yet."

The timing is now. It is time to create what is stirring in our hearts and bodies. It is getting ready to crack out of the egg, to sprout forth from the ground, to be born from our souls now that excuses and routine tasks, work and school, and social obligations are cleared away.

It's time to write the thing, paint the thing, feel the thing, express the thing in whatever way it's coming through. We know our lives cannot be the same after this. We know we must do things differently. We know this starts with right now. *How are we showing up to ourselves* right now? *We can no longer travel outside of ourselves. For the foreseeable future, it's time to travel within.*

Chapter Nine
SEPTEMBER

"I am the mother, I nurture all of creation."

IN SEPTEMBER, we celebrate the Autumn Equinox, a balance point between the heat and transformation of summer and quiet rest of winter. As the second of the harvest festivals, it is a time to receive the blessings of Earth, nurture our bodies and the world around us, and celebrate the abundance in our lives with gratitude.

Receptivity ♦ Nurture ♦ Abundance ♦ Gratitude

The Mother

The Mother is the originator and nurturer of all human life, yet she is one of the most disregarded and abused roles in our current dominant culture. The power of the Mother is to nurture new life into existence and give of her energy and life force to do so. When there is balance, the Mother receives nurturing and life force from her community while she is growing the life within her. She invites us to look at our relationship to giving and receiving, as both are needed to maintain the creative power within us. The Mother also reminds us of the abundance of the Earth. When the Mother is nourished, all life is nourished. There is plenty for all to be deeply nourished and loved. We give gratitude to the Earth as our original Mother, provider of all our needs and desires—offering gratitude is also an act of giving and receiving.

The Wound: Unworthiness

The Healing: Receiving

Element: Fire/Water

Plant Ally: Cinnamon
Cinnamon is warming, energizing, and embodies abundance in love and material wealth. It brings a depth and richness to life while also being sweet and comforting.

Animal Ally: Bear
Bear honors the rhythm of the seasons and goes into hibernation during the dark months for rest and introspection. She is fiercely protective of her young and will stand in her power when needed, but also allow space for softness, play, and deep rest. Bear understands the cycles of reciprocity: when to give and when to receive.

Stone Ally: Turquoise
This stone is inherently soothing and nurturing, grounding us lovingly and beautifully. Turquoise can also be worked with to reduce stress and pain, and create freedom from emotional bondage.

Monthly Themes

Receptivity is the action of allowing creation to unfold in our lives, rather than making things happen. It is being open to the blessings the Earth is offering and filling our cups, so they overflow to bring abundance to others. In reciprocity, as we receive so must we give to keep the energy, wisdom, and gifts of the Universe flowing to others. When we are unable to receive, we cannot be generous or nurture the world.

Nurture: The Mother archetype nurtures new life into being and nourishes the new life with her body so it will grow. Her unconditional love helps the new life thrive. The Mother archetype sets the example for how to walk in the world with grace, power, and kindness. We must learn to nurture ourselves first, because so many of our mothers were expected to give and nurture without receiving. After the energy and work of spring and summer, autumn moves us into a time of replenishment as we say goodbye to the high energy of the sun and begin welcoming the peace of the darkness. Autumn is the invitation to tend to the Self, and bring attention back to hearth and home, nesting and beautifying our spaces, and eating nourishing foods.

Abundance is a law of the universe. Mother Earth creates abundantly, and as her creations, so do we. Earth's abundance is in the fields of dandelion flowers in spring, the juniper berries ripening at the end of summer, and the leaves that are shed each autumn, which allow for the abundance of new growth to come next spring. When we understand this concept at work in our lives, we can be more intentional about the kind of abundance we welcome into our lives. From our current programming, we create an abundance of fear, scarcity, drama, and distractions—now is the time to conceptualize true abundance of resources for all, connection, love, peace, truth, and support from Spirit. When we acknowledge the abundance in our lives, we create space for more.

Gratitude is the most powerful practice we can use when calling abundance into our lives. It is the other side of reciprocity, and it benefits both the giver and receiver. It raises our vibration and states to the universe: "Yes, thank you, more please!" It reminds us of our place in the world and our relationship to everything around us so we can be in harmony with that abundance.

Affirmations

I am blessed.

I am grateful.

I am generous.

I receive abundance with ease and joy.

I have all I need to create the life I want.

My personal affirmations:

_____
_____
_____
_____

Daily Invocation

Spirit, thank you for this new day. May I receive all your blessings with an open heart. Where I feel lack, help me see abundance. Today, I will nurture myself with love and patience. When I feel lost and alone, support and encourage me. Show me connectivity in all things. Show me where I can nurture new life in the world. Help me to feel true gratitude and express it freely. Blessed Be.

My personal intentions and prayers:

_____
_____
_____
_____
_____
_____
_____
_____

Tending to the Womb-space Meditation

Ground into your breath to wake up all the cells of your body. Root your energy into the Earth and call on your higher Self to support you in this meditation. Begin to breathe into your womb space. Notice the quality of this area. What sensations, images, and emotions arise as you offer your loving awareness in your womb space. Take a moment to be fully present, breathing deeply into the experience. Breathe healing golden light from your heart into your womb space. Imagine through the breath that you are bringing supportive loving energy from the Earth through your roots. A beautiful green light spreads up your legs and into your womb space. See the meeting of the golden and green energies filling this space with fertile, loving energy.

Now imagine a spark of creation coming alive in your womb space, nurtured by the green light from the Earth and the golden light from your heart. You are receiving all you need to allow this spark of life to grow. You can imagine this as something new you are seeking to call forth in your life or something that is in your life now that you wish to nourish more deeply. Feel it growing and thriving. Feel it stirring in preparation to come forth into the world. Imagine it being lovingly birthed from your body, still swathed in the golden-green light of nourishment. Feel the energy moving through and out of you abundantly, coming through the Earth and you, and out of you with ease and joy. See yourself nourishing this life as it grows and grows and begins to create its own nourishment to thrive. Feel the green and golden energy returning to you, filling, nourishing, and replenishing you. Offer thanks to the Earth, your body, and the beautiful creation that has come forth from you.

Reflections on this meditation:

_____
_____
_____
_____
_____
_____
_____
_____
_____
_____
_____
_____

Card Spread

-1-
What are my blocks to abundance and receiving in my life now?

-2-
What supports me in receiving abundance?

-3-
What areas of my life need nurturing right now?

-4-
How is Spirit supporting me in this?

Journal Prompts

Choose one or more of these questions each week to reflect and explore here or in your journal.

What is my relationship to receiving? How do I experience this in my body?

How do I nurture myself and others? Where is more nurturance needed?

Where do I perceive abundance in my life today? Where do I perceive lack?

How do I express gratitude?

Where do I resist receiving nurturance in my life? What makes it difficult for me to receive?

When I am open to receive, what happens for me? How can I open myself up to more receptivity?

What would abundance look like for me in my life right now? How have I made space for abundance in my life?

What am I most grateful for in my life?

How can I nurture myself and others in ways that feel life-giving to me?

List five to ten favorite self-care skills and commit to practicing them for the remainder of the year.

Monthly Rituals

Ritual Tea

- 1 part cinnamon
- 1 part elderberry
- 1 part rosehip
- ½ part fresh ginger

Combine everything in a small pot and simmer for 15 minutes. Strain and add honey to taste.

Ritual Full Moon Bath

Make a warming spicy infusion of cinnamon, ginger, clove, and rose petals by simmering in fresh water for about 15 minutes. Strain and add a spoonful of honey (you can use your abundance honey from your Lughnasa celebration, see Page 146) and a cup of milk. Add to a warm bath. As you bathe, reflect on what needs nurturing and warmth in your life, allowing it to be infused with the energy of the water. Connect with the areas that already feel nurtured and abundant. Offer gratitude to yourself for this deeply nourishing practice.

New Moon Candle Spell

Using a yellow or green candle, anoint with Triple Rose oil (see Page 44) and sprinkle lightly with ground cinnamon. Speak to the flame about where you are needing more receptivity, more nurturing, and more abundance into your life. Bring the energy of your intentions into your body, beginning in the heart space, feeling yourself embody your intentions. Feel your intentions grow from your heart space out to the rest of your body, until your whole body glows with this warming flame. Offer gratitude and let the candle burn all the way down.

Practice: Daily Gratitude

Commit to a daily gratitude practice this month. Either write in your journal or state the gratitudes out loud, list three to five things you are grateful for each day. This is a lovely practice to do with the family around the dinner table, or a quiet journal practice to do each evening before bed.

Reflections:

What do I notice when I practice gratitude daily?

What new blessings have come since doing this practice?

What blessings have always been there that I now see more clearly?

How can I integrate this gratitude practice into my daily life moving forward?

Create an appreciation jar:
A beautiful way to keep our thoughts centered in gratitude and strengthen the foundations of our relationships is by acknowledging what we appreciate in others. Find a large mason jar or other container (an old coffee can or a small box). Cut a slit in the top to put in your appreciations. Have everyone in your household commit to writing daily, weekly, or monthly appreciations for everyone else in the home and put them in the jar. Keep a pad of paper and pen close by or attach it to your box to help you remember. Designate a time each year (or seasonally) to open your jar and read the appreciations out loud to others or yourself.

Practice: Create a Pentacle

Create a Pentacle for your home to cultivate the nurturing, loving, and abundant energies in your space.

Pentacles are used to represent the Earth element, as well as the unification of all the elements (5 points representing Earth, Air, Fire, Water, and Spirit). It is a grounding and nurturing symbol. Work with it to represent protection, material wealth and security, and magic. Folks used to infuse their home décor with intentions; this is a revival of that ancient practice. There are many ways to make a pentacle for your home, these are just simple suggestions. Follow your desires and unique creativity. That's what makes it potent magic for you!

On a piece of paper, write what magic you want your pentacle to hold for your home space. Some ideas are: protection, connection, unconditional love, harmony, personal power, joy and laughter, abundance, and security.

Two ways to create your pentacle:

1. Take a walk in nature and gather sticks from the ground approximately the same length (or cut/snap them so they are the same length). You will need 5 sticks total. Back at home, shape the sticks into a five-pointed star and tie or glue the corners together. This is your pentacle!
2. Go to the craft store and buy ribbon, lace, yarn, or twine, and a wreath of branches already tied together. Wrap the ribbon around your wreath in a star shape, so that the pentacle is in the center of the wreath (like a dream catcher, but witchy). Glue the ribbon in place.

Decorate either of these with beads and charms. Glue the decorations onto your pentacle/wreath or hang them from strips of ribbon or twine at the bottom. Some ideas:

- Add clear quartz for clarity of vision, communication, and intentions
- Add smoky quartz to repel negativity and doubt
- Citrine for abundance
- Bells to clear the air and raise the vibration
- Add greenery from around your home or that is native to the place you live: juniper sprigs, sagebrush, rowan berries, or cedar boughs. Ask for permission of the Plant Spirits before harvesting, and leave an offering to the Plant Spirit. Connect with the medicine of the plant to align your intentions with your pentacle.

Make your pentacle as elaborate or as simple as you like. Hang the pentacle over your front door to remind you of your intentions and allow its magic to influence anyone who enters your home.

Celebrate Autumn Equinox/Mabon!

September 21st–23rd in Northern Hemisphere
March 21st–23rd in Southern Hemisphere

Once again, the Autumn Equinox brings us back to a balance point of our year, where the length of our days and nights are equal. This is a powerful time to reflect on what feels balanced in our lives and what areas are asking for more balance. What do you need to create balance as you enter the colder, darker months of fall and winter? Autumn is commonly associated with the element of Water—this month we will consecrate a cauldron to connect with the element of Water and open ourselves to its wisdom.

Often depicted with a cauldron is the Welsh goddess, Cerridwen. She created a potion in her cauldron to make her son wise, but her assistant accidentally took the potion instead. In her anger, she chased him down. Both the assistant and Cerridwen changed forms several times until the assistant turned himself into a single grain, and Cerridwen, as a hen, ate him. Then she became pregnant and gave birth to him. Cerridwen invites us to examine what we put in our cauldron of creation. She also embodies a mother archetype, which is fitting for September's theme. She is a goddess of transformation, wisdom, magic, and creation. To honor Cerridwen on your Equinox altar, place a small cauldron or cup filled with grain or seeds. You can also charge your Creativity Spell bag on your altar alongside your offering as she is also a goddess of creativity and inspiration.

The coming of autumn also welcomes element of Water: flowing intuition, reflection, deep healing, and emotional release. Here are some thoughts on working with the element of water and the season of autumn.

Season: Autumn

Element: Water

Tarot: Suit of cups

Direction: West

Time of day: Dusk

Symbology: Introspection, intuition, and flow

Body: Heart

Magical tools: water (in all forms), blood, oil, potions and teas, chalice, bowl, cauldron

Take time to meditate and journal about what water represents for you. How water resonates for you will be how it's most potent in your magic. What memories are associated with water? How would you embody water? How does water move, speak, or exert its will? What do you love about water? How does water heal you? What does water reflect to you?

Feel what it's like to communicate and work with the element of Water. Think of it as a relationship you are cultivating. Be open to how water responds to you and what it wants from you.

Cauldron consecration

A witch's cauldron is a powerful tool in our magic. It is where our spells and intentions simmer, swirl, and transform in the alchemy of Earth and Spirit. Cooking pots that have been passed down from our elders are wonderful kitchen cauldrons, or invest in a nice pot that you will use forever. You can also get a traditional cast iron witch's cauldron. Choose a cauldron that feels powerful and significant for you. It can even be a teacup!

To consecrate a cauldron means to make it a sacred object. You can consecrate all magical tools (and I recommend you do as it suits you). Once the cauldron is consecrated, treat it with respect and cultivate a relationship with it. I cook all my healing stews and broths in my kitchen cauldron and put my intentions into everything I make into it. I take good care of the cauldron and offer it gratitude.

This ritual will consecrate your cauldron to amplify and support your magic.

You will need:
- A cauldron of your choosing
- Incense or your wand
- A candle or small fire outdoors
- Triple Rose Oil, or any sacred oil or holy water
- A pinch of sea salt

1. Create your sacred space by cleansing your energy and casting a circle.
2. Pass smoke or your wand over the cauldron as you speak:
   Powers of air, vision, and light
   Bless this cauldron with sacred sight.
3. Add your salt to the bowl and say:
   Powers of Earth, rock, and bone
   Bless this cauldron as sacred ground.
4. Anoint with your Triple Rose Oil or water and say:
   Powers of water, blood, and oil
   Bless this cauldron with sacred flow.

5. Place the cauldron over the flame and say:
   Powers of fire, heat, and sun
   Bless this cauldron with transformation.
   By the power of three times three. Blessed be. Blessed be. Blessed be.

(This incantation can be adapted any way you like. It is your magic!)

When your cauldron is consecrated, close your circle. You can charge your cauldron on your altar for the Equinox and leave offerings to Cerridwen in the cauldron. Ask her to bless it as well.

Prepare for the Next Celebration!

Samhain is also referred to as All Hallows Eve and All Saints Day and can be celebrated from October 30th to November 1st in the Northern Hemisphere and April 30th to May 1st in the Southern Hemisphere, depending on your personal traditions. For many witches, it is the most important holiday of the year and often referred to as the "Witches New Year."

Items to prepare, gather, and/or place on your altar:
- Pumpkins and gourds
- Lanterns
- Black candles
- Photographs of and objects connected to your ancestors
- Food and drink offerings to your ancestors
- Your witchiest outfits: cloaks, pointed hats, black and purple velvet, anything that makes you feel powerful and magical
- Divination objects: tarot cards, runes, crystal balls, and scrying mirrors, and pendulums *(I personally do not practice with Ouija boards, but include them if they are part of your practice)*
- Skulls and bones
- Garlic, red wine, keys, and honey to offer Hecate

Monthly Reflections

What was most challenging for me this month?
___
___

What was most rewarding? What growth have I witnessed in myself?
___
___

Magical associations to the Mother:
___
___

Tree, herb, flower, and plant allies I worked with:
___
___

Animal allies I worked with:
___
___

Stone allies I worked with:

Songs:

Scents:

Food and drink:

People, Deities, Role Models:

My Personal Practices: *What am I learning about my personal magic through these practices?*

Mother

Ocean Mother is
Cleansing power, fierce movement
Churning loving waves

Forest Mother is
Soothing quiet, growth and death
Peaceful loving heart

Mountain Mother is
Protective, strong and stable
Constant rooted love

Desert Mother is
Teacher guide showing ourselves
What is possible

Mother loves deeply
Abundantly; joyfully
All returns to her

Chapter Ten
OCTOBER

"I am a Witch. I transform in darkness."

IN OCTOBER, as the world around us dies away, we settle into the coming dark season and go deeper within to rest, reflect, and integrate what we've learned in previous months. This is a beautiful time to honor the Witch archetype and take time to explore our shadow, shame, and Witch wound.

Shadow ✦ Death ✦ Intuition ✦ Transformation

THE WITCH

The Witch has long been maligned as an evil force. There is a long history of naming powerful women as witches as an excuse to strip them of their power and eliminate their power through torture or death (many men and children were also accused and punished as witches). In reclaiming the name *Witch*, as a mirror for yourself, you align with your power, magic, and shadow selves. All of us have a history or lineage fraught with pain, trauma, and darkness. We cannot bypass these truths of who we are. Instead, we are invited to release our shame and reintegrate the gifts of our history to be whole and rooted in the truth of who we are. Accepting our truths helps us be intentional and mindful and not perpetuate the harm we carry from our legacies onto others or ourselves.

THE WOUND: Shame

THE HEALING: Embracing our shadow

ELEMENT: Water

PLANT ALLY: Rosemary
Rosemary is one of the most powerful and versatile plant allies, enhancing our magic with potency but remaining very down to Earth. It is an herb of remembrance, helping us remember who we are, where we came from, and the people who matter most. It is also a funerary herb, honoring that which has died away. Rosemary gives clarity, cleansing, and purification to the body and our environment. It is a most basic and invaluable witch's helper.

ANIMAL ALLY: Raven
Dark as night, Ravens are symbols of mystery and death, shapeshifters, wisdom keepers, and tricksters. Sometimes seen as harbingers of evil or bad omens, the Raven is a powerful ally for embracing the shadow self and the season of death for transformation.

STONE ALLY: Labradorite
A powerful ally in shadow work, labradorite helps us access our deep intuitive wisdom. It acts as a loving reflector of all facets of ourselves and encourages us to see the beauty in them all.

Montly Themes

Our shadow is a potent teacher of what does not serve us and can be transformed to support our growth through new ways being born. We are taught to fear and suppress our shadow, which only serves to distort and strengthen its power to manifest through our subconscious that which we do not want. When we make friends with our shadow, we learn how to be in loving relationship with the parts of ourselves that haven't been seen, loved, or honored. We work with our shadow to help us create light. The Witch archetype has lived in the shadows for a very long time; this doesn't make her evil. It only makes her gifts and powers less accessible to us. Let us bring her out of the shadows to harness her wisdom.

Death is a part of life that we may fear but is completely unavoidable. When we get comfortable with death, we welcome the transformation that comes from it. Death is freedom and release from old, outdated ways of being and brings quiet and rest so new things can begin to be conceived. Through the decay and transformation of that which no longer serves, Death gives nourishment for new life.

Intuition comes from the quiet within. We must clear away the old debris, our fears, attachments, and stories to allow our inner wisdom to speak to us and guide us into the next phase of conception, birth, and life. We must practice making the time to get quiet and honor the inner guidance we receive, so our intuition communicates clearly.

Transformation is what happens when the snake sheds its old skin, the sun sets and rises again, and the cauldron of dreams is stirred. We release old desires, stories, and woundings, and step into a new way of being. It happens through surrender, acceptance, and trust.

Affirmations

I am a light in the darkness. I do not fear my shadow.

I allow experiences of pain and shame to teach me what is ready to be released now.

I release all that does not serve me.

I hear and trust my intuition with clarity and confidence.

I am transforming into my highest expression of self.

My personal affirmations:

_____

_____

_____

_____

Daily Invocation

Spirit, I trust that I am on the path of transformation to be in the fullest expression of who I am meant to be on this planet at this time. Show me what is dying away and allow me to transform. Help me face death with courage and faith. Help me love and honor the parts of me that are dying away. Help me understand my shadow so I can work with it, not against it. Activate my intuition and give me confidence to trust myself and follow the guidance of my inner voice. Help me hear that voice clearly. Spirit, walk with me when I feel afraid, shame overcomes me, or I want to run from my pain. Bring me healing and peace. Help me step fully into my power and magic by embracing all parts of who I am. Blessed Be.

My personal intentions and prayers:

_____

_____

_____

_____

_____

_____

_____

Inner Wise Woman Meditation

In a quiet place where you will not be disturbed, sit or lie comfortably. Bring your awareness to your breath and body. Take three deep relaxing breaths and root your energy into Mother Earth. Ask for her assistance and support in connecting with your intuition. Scan your body and breathe into any areas of tension or holding. Encourage your body to relax.

Think of an area of your life that is lacking clarity. When you bring this experience forth in your awareness, notice what happens in your body. If your lack of clarity were a place in nature, what would it look like? Let it take shape in your mind's eye, perhaps as a tangled forest, a fierce hurricane, or maybe it's like a superhighway with cars zooming by so fast it is all a blur. Allow your lack of clarity to take shape however it wants. Don't force it or try to control how it looks. Let whatever feelings come to wash over you.

Now say to yourself: *"I invite my Inner Wise Woman to show me the way. I am open to the understanding and guidance from my inner knowing."* Imagine a dark tunnel opening in front of you. Enter the tunnel, and leave the chaos and intensity behind. The tunnel is completely silent and still. It descends into your psyche, deeper and deeper. As you descend into the tunnel, you see a faint light glowing in the distance. It gets closer and closer until you see a woman holding a lantern, illuminating the darkness that surrounds you both. She is your Inner Wise Woman. Notice how she shows up for you, what she looks like, and the energy she carries. She is the part of you who is eternal and has already seen the entire course of your life. She knows which way to go.

As you approach her, she smiles and reaches her hand to you. You take her hand and continue down the tunnel together. She leads you into a cozy chamber, with a warm fire blazing in a stone hearth and a soft sofa in front of the fireplace. She sits you down and lovingly wraps you in blankets and offers you a cup of tea to warm your bones. Your Inner Wise Woman sits with you on the sofa and puts her hand to your heart, looking deeply into your eyes.

Allow her wisdom to be revealed to you. Ask her any questions and receive her wisdom through her touch or look. Be open to any knowing that comes to you.

Stay with your wise woman as long as you like. Feel her energy so you can call on it anytime. When you feel complete, thank your Inner Wise Woman, and offer gratitude to Mother Earth, pick up her lantern, and walk back up the tunnel, returning to where you are sitting in meditation. Write in your journal to reflect on your experience with your Inner Wise Woman.

Once you have done this meditation, make a commitment to call on your Wise Woman daily. Imagine yourself tuning into her energy and wisdom.

Reflections on this meditation:

CARD SPREAD

-1-
What part of my shadow is asking to be seen?

-2-
How can I love and heal my shadow?

-3-
How can I deeply attune to my intuition?

-4-
What transformation will I experience through my shadow work?

Journal Prompts

Choose one or more of these questions each week to reflect and explore here or in your journal.

What is my relationship to my shadow? What thoughts, feelings, and sensations arise when I reflect on my shadow self?

What do I fear most about my shadow? What do I feel most ashamed of?

How can I create a loving space for my shadow to come forth? What would it say to me?

As I navigate my shadow work, what do I notice arising in me? What is ready to die/be released?

What is asking to be witnessed in my shadow work? How do I feel about serving as a witness to this part of myself?

How does my intuition communicate with me? How do I feel it in my body?

What support from Spirit do I need when examining my shadow self? How can I support myself in this work?

What transformations are happening for me right now? What transformations do I wish for?

Monthly Rituals

Ritual Tea Blend

This chai is especially luxurious and smooth made with half water and half milk.

- 1 part black tea or rooibos
- ½ part dried rosemary
- ½ part fennel seed
- ½ part cinnamon chips
- 6 pods cardamom
- ¼ whole cloves

Crush all spices (except the tea) in a mortar and pestle. Combine everything in a small pot with the water and milk. Simmer for 15 minutes, turn off heat, and allow to steep for another 5 minutes before straining and adding honey.

Full Moon Ritual Bath

To a running bath, add one cup of Epsom or sea salt, three sprigs of rosemary and a pinch of your Witch's Black Salt or a spoonful of ground charcoal. You can also add a few drops of rosemary essential oil, if desired. As you soak, call on the clarity of the rosemary and vision of the Raven to guide you in seeing yourself more clearly. Feel yourself embracing all parts of you with strength and acceptance. *The charcoal may leave some residue on the bath tub but shouldn't stain it.*

New Moon Candle Spell

Anoint a black candle with Triple Rose oil and sprinkle with dried rosemary. Gaze into the flame, and call on your inner Witch. How does she appear to you? What does she want from you? What must you release to allow her to stand in her power? Give any obstacles, resistance, and shadows to the flame and welcome the Witch into you. Feel her activating in the cells of your body.

Practice: Personal Power Potion and Shadow Integration

Put your intentions into water by making a potion. Water holds memory and information. Our bodies are filled with our intentions whether we know it or not. Potions are a very simple, fun, and a potent way to work with intention and bring them into your body or embody them. Some ideas to play with: speak your intentions, sing, whisper, or shout them with joy into your morning tea/coffee or anything else you cook with water, such as broth or soups. Also, you can bless the water by ringing bells, blowing kisses, dancing over it, giving blessings, or leaving offerings. Infuse your intentions in your drinking water by putting crystals infused with your intentions and energy. *Make sure the crystals are water safe or use a water bottle specifically designed to hold crystals.*

This potion is designed to help you connect with your shadow work. Our shadow is not what is "bad" about us. It is the parts of us we have hidden away—oftentimes those can be quite positive! If at any point we feared or were given the message that something beautiful about us was unacceptable, it's likely that this element of who we are got pushed into the shadows. Begin with this journaling exercise to connect with all parts of you:

Journal prompts: a personal inventory

List ten traits about yourself that you perceive as negative.

List ten traits about yourself that you perceive as positive.

List at least three things about yourself that are hidden/unseen by others—parts of yourself that you have hidden away.

List at least three things that other people admire about you.

Gather these herbs and crystals to concoct your power potion

- Rose – connection to Divine, high vibration, self-love, and healing
- Damiana – sexy witchy power, desire, creation, femininity, beauty
- Lemon Balm – healing, soothing, nurturing, supportive
- Chamomile – healing, sun energy, abundance, soothing
- Hibiscus – love and passion, desire
- Cinnamon – attraction, spice and fire, desire, abundance
- Cacao nibs – heart opener, connection to higher self, embodiment, balance of masculine and feminine energy, creativity, and joy
- Clear Quartz - purity and clarity of intention
- Amethyst crystals - personal power, self-acceptance, beauty

1. Do a ritual cleansing of yourself and your space and cast a circle.
2. In your cauldron, add fresh spring water. Put in your small clear quartz or amethyst crystals when the water is still cool. Begin to heat your cauldron on the stove or a ritual fire. Add your herbs one-by-one. Speak your intentions for each herb or crystal as you drop them in the water.
3. As your potion begins to simmer, speak into it:
   I ask my angels, guides, and ancestors to imbue me with power to see myself wholly.
   Show me my fears so I may face them with courage
   Help me use my shortcomings as strengths
   and my strengths with wisdom and integrity.
   Help me see all of me, that I am beautiful, powerful, and magical in all ways.
   Help me love myself as I am, so I may love others.
4. Now read your personal inventory aloud to the potion. See your reflection as it moves on the surface of the water. See all parts of you as gifts and helpers in your personal magic. Strain your potion, add honey, and drink. Welcome all of the parts of yourself back into your body with love, reverence, and gratitude.
5. Close your circle and journal about your experience. Cleanse your crystals and your cauldron and give the spent herbs back to the Earth (bury them or put them in your compost).

Practice: Scrying

Scrying is a form of divination that activates and hones our intuitive abilities. It uses a reflective surface such as a mirror or water (fire gazing is also considered scrying) to open our "third eye" and access our inner knowing. Think of scrying as looking at the clouds and seeing shapes in them. We all see different things based on what's happening for us internally. It is a way our intuition speaks to us if we can get quiet and still enough to hear it.

To practice scrying, fill your cauldron with water. You can use a mirror or do this with any body of water such as a river, lake, or well. Find a dark, quiet spot where you will not be interrupted. For protection and focusing your intention, cast a circle, and call on your guides to assist you. Light a candle to provide enough light to see its gentle reflections on the water. Do a grounding meditation (see Page 23) and connect with what you wish to see or understand in your scrying. Look into the surface of the water and soften your gaze, as if you were looking beyond the water. Tune into your body and notice sensations, feelings, thoughts, and insights that arise. Notice if any reflections remind you of anything—animals, people, objects—similar to how you might look at symbols in a dream (we will explore dream work in December). The more often you scry, the better you'll get. When you are finished, journal about your experience, symbols you saw, and the sensations in your body. Close your circle and offer gratitude for the knowledge you've received.

Celebrate Samhain!

October 31st - Nov 1st in the Northern Hemisphere
April 30th - May 1st in the Southern Hemisphere

Samhain is often referred to as the Witches New Year. During this holiday, the veil between worlds thins and makes your magic potent in the Spiritual realms. It is a time of celebrating your magic and power, courageously facing your shadow, and burning your fears, limitations, and old stories in the fire. All Saint's Day on November 1st is a time to honor your ancestors, and connect with souls and spirits that support you. Give them thanks and ask for their guidance and assistance in your personal journeys.

Hecate is an ancient Greek Goddess representing magic and witchcraft. She carries a lantern and stands at the crossroads between the worlds. Hecate helps us navigate the shadows within ourselves. She is often a helper of lost souls and assists those who have been cast out. She shows us how to lovingly and powerfully reclaim the parts of ourselves that we have hidden to stay safe, not to fear the darkness, and light the way for others. *Offerings for Hecate:* wine, garlic, keys, honey, and candles/lanterns.

Fire release ritual

This is a very simple version of a fire release. You are welcome to add or change anything you like. You can do this ritual alone or with a group.

1. Begin by cleansing your energy, either with a ritual salt bath or with smoke from burning herbs or incense.
2. Set your space. You will need either a black candle or a fire pit if you are doing it outside with a group. You will also need paper and pen.
3. Cast your circle (see Page 64). Delineate the sacred space with salt, your wand, or both. Call in the directions and your guides for support and assistance.
4. Light your fire or your candle.
5. With your pen and paper, write all that you are ready to release, is dying away, your fears, obstacles, negative and unloving thoughts and patterns, old stories that no longer apply, toxic relationships, painful memories, regrets, resentments, or anything that feels stuck.
6. When you've written everything and feel complete, speak your words into the fire, start with the words: *"I release..."*
7. Once you have spoken your releases out loud, put the paper into the fire, allowing it to burn and transform.
8. When you are complete, offer gratitude to yourself, your guides, the fire, the Earth, and the directions, and close your circle.
9. Take a cleansing shower or sprinkle yourself with water that has been blessed to remove all residual energy from your release work.

Monthly Reflections

What was most challenging for me this month?

What was most rewarding? What growth have I witnessed in myself?

Magical associations to the Witch:

Tree, herb, flower, and plant allies I worked with:

Animal allies I worked with:

Stone allies I worked with:

Songs:

Scents:

Food and drink:

People, Deities, Role Models:

My Personal Practices: *What am I learning about my personal magic through these practices?*

Shadow Monster

My shadow slowly emerges from her dark, hidden places. Today, I see her in my exhaustion, in the piles of clothes at the foot of my bed, waiting to be folded and put away.

She is 14 years old. And she is 9 years old, and 22 years old. She stands with a massive shaggy monster, her protector. Sometimes the monster walks behind her. Sometimes she hides herself in the long strands of his fur, tightly holding him to dissolve herself out of the world. She likes to run away from things. She likes hiding and being invisible.

She is very lonely, but for her shaggy companion. She does not trust the Earth under her feet or the authority figures who are supposed to help her and keep her safe. She is constantly free falling into nothing, darkness, and oblivion. It is her only escape from the life of chaos that is before her.

She prefers to keep others at a distance, and doesn't show herself because she doesn't quite know herself. She feels competitive and judgmental of others, especially other females. She wants to win, and knows she is losing.

She likes to numb. Her shadow's preferred numbing mechanism is through smoke; tobacco and cannabis, a deeper memory of a loving relationship to medicinal plants turned to the only access to plant medicine through substances that change how she feels. Even when it makes her feel poorly, it's at least a slight shift from alone, afraid, angry, and lost.

She likes to feel the ache of exhaustion in her bones. She likes being sick because it means she gets to rest and focus on herself for a bit. And maybe others will focus on her, too, for a little while. Maybe not.

She likes being poor for it shows her grit, defines her "otherness," declares to the world that she doesn't give a fuck about system of privilege and power, except when she does.

She does not believe that men know how to take care of things, or of people. She does not believe that anyone knows how to take care of her, nor that they want to. She believes she is on her own. Falling.

She resents success, brilliance, laughter, freedom, and power. It shines on her so brightly it hurts, reminding her of all the things she is not, and cannot be.

I have hated her, my shadow. I have blamed her for my stuckness, my exhaustion, my smallness, and my fear of her power. Hating her has only made her hate me more.

I look at the clothes to be folded, the symbol of all the ways I feel I am failing. I take a breath. My shadow asks for love, compassion, and patience. She cannot change who she is. When I love her, I get up and fold the damn clothes. When I love her, I say: today we do not choose fear and smallness and resentment. *When I love her, I let her rest, heal, and forgive herself.*

CHAPTER ELEVEN
NOVEMBER

"I am the dreams of my ancestors. I mourn the pain of the Earth."

NOVEMBER DEEPENS our connection to the darkness and death. It is a time to honor the dead, mourn our losses, and crack open our hearts to fierce compassion. So much of our culture seeks to avoid pain and messiness. This month we'll look gently at the pain and suffering of our ancestors and allow their grief to be witnessed and released as we transform our collective story.

GRIEF ✦ MOURNING ✦ COMPASSION ✦ ANCESTORS

The Grieving Woman

The Grieving Woman is a part of us that many seek to avoid or deny, as her process is messy, painful, and scary. But the truth is we all experience loss and grief. We all have stories of pain in our ancestral lineages. When we look at the truth of our pain in this lifetime and our ancestral histories, the Grieving Woman archetype shows us the gifts, lessons, and deepening wisdom of grief. Our scars are our strength; they make it possible to hold space for the pain of others. These wounds teach us what dangers to avoid. They show us our resilience and bind us together in solidarity.

The Wound: Denying our pain

The Healing: Honoring our pain

Element: Water

Plant Ally: Mullein
Mullein is deeply soothing to the lungs, a place in our bodies where we hold grief. This plant ally supports our breath, which helps us move through grief and expand our capacity to tolerate deep sadness and loss.

Animal Ally: Whale
Whales have been observed mourning their dead, a trait not common in most members of the animal kingdom. Whales are wisdom keepers, ancient and intelligent. The spirit of the Whale can guide and soothe us in moving through our grief and connecting with the ancient wisdom of our ancestors.

Stone Ally: Smoky Quartz
This stone absorbs negativity and brings soothing energy to wired, frayed, and intense emotions. If you are ruminating in negativity, work with smoky quartz to ease grief and filter the negative energy of others.

Monthly Themes

Grief is the natural response to loss and death. There is so much dying away in our world, so much pain is asking to be witnessed. Before we jump to "moving on" from grief, we must learn to hold space for it. Avoiding this discomfort cuts us off from the wisdom that comes from death, the lessons of our painful experiences and those of our ancestors. Denying or avoiding grief denies us the gift of connecting to the other realms. Through the depths of our grief, we gain the resilience to embody our spiritual power.

Mourning with ourselves and our communities is how we express and honor our grief. There is much to mourn as the old systems die away: the pain and oppression experienced by folks who have been marginalized and abused by a dominant culture, our separation from our divinity and inner wisdom, the trauma of our ancestors, and all the ways we continue to be unloving to ourselves, others, and the Earth. Mourning is the balm to our broken hearts. It is the witness that allows us to receive and integrate the lessons that come from this pain, suffering, and loss, keeping us present in our experience and in our bodies, so pain and trauma don't get stuck inside.

Compassion comes after we feel our pain fully. We begin to understand and develop profound empathy for others' pain. In grief, we are connected. When we feel the intensity of our pain, we can see the places in the world that perpetuate harmful ways of being that are unnecessary and require transformation. When we've walked through the darkness of our pain, we become fearless, for we know our capacity to heal. We understand true resilience. We become willing to walk through the fire for our fellow beings. Until all of us are free, none of us are free.

Ancestors. The ancestors of our lineage and the land beneath our feet are allies in our spiritual work. We ask these bright and benevolent ancestors to assist us in this time of personal and global evolution. Throughout our history and dominant culture, we have been cut off from accessing ancestral wisdom, emphasizing only that which is new, young, and innovative. Some of us come from lineages that have been historically oppressed, tortured, and dehumanized. Others come from those who inflicted this pain and trauma. So many of us come from both. When we avoid the depth of this pain, we bypass the work that is needed to remedy these transgressions on humanity. We perpetuate the wounds. When we connect with our ancestors, there is much wisdom and healing to be gained. They are ready to show up for us now. Our healing is also healing them, and vice versa.

Affirmations

I welcome sorrow as a gateway to healing.

I tend to my heart when I am grieving.

I am always guided and supported by my ancestors.

I am resilient. I am compassionate.

My personal affirmations:

_____
_____
_____
_____

Daily Invocation

Spirit, hold me today as I make space for grief. Show me the light through the darkness. Allow me to trust that my pain will pass. Help me honor the people and ways of being that have passed from this world, creating space for new relationships and ways of being. Help me tend to my weeping heart. Ancestors, bright and benevolent, share with me your wisdom. Show me how to be resilient in the face of my pain. Show me how to love others in their pain. Let my compassion be light in the darkness for others in the world. Blessed be.

My personal intentions and prayers:

_____
_____
_____
_____
_____
_____
_____
_____

Welcoming the Ancestors Meditation

Begin by grounding into your breath and bring awareness to your body. Root your breath into the Earth and invite your higher Self to support you during this meditation. As you breathe, send your root energy farther and farther into the Earth. See your energy dropping through the floor, the soil and rock beneath you, the water table, the crystals and ancient fossils and caverns, through the magma, all the way to the center of the Earth. As you arrive in the belly of the Earth, in a cavern illuminated with a ritual fire, you walk closer to the fire and hear the beating of drums. You see bodies around the fire, their faces turned toward the flames. As you get closer, the drumming intensifies. The circle of bodies around the fire opens, and you take your place in the circle. The light of the fire shows you the faces of your bright and benevolent ancestors. They welcome you to their sacred gathering. They embrace you, smiling, patting you on the back, and celebrating you. Receive their warmth and welcome. Return to the arms of your ancestors. The fire warms your skin and the pulse of the drums beat deep in your heart. Once they have welcomed you, your ancestors dance around the fire. They invite you to join them. Allow your body to move freely, dancing with the people who have walked before you. Know they have always been with you. Your blood moves quickly as you feel their power pulsing through your veins. Receive their power and move your body as it moves you. The gifts of your ancestors fill you. Their wisdom activates their love and guidance in your bones. Allow your cells to absorb your ancestors' gifts and bring the heat of the fire into your body. Your body, mind, and spirit fill with gratitude and a deep remembering of who you are, and from whom you come.

When you feel complete, offer gratitude to the fire, your ancestors, the Earth, and your higher Self. Keep the memory of your ancestors inside your body, travel back to the surface of the Earth, returning to your room. Take a deep breath. You are complete.

Reflections on this meditation:

Card Spread

-1- What grief am I holding today?

-2- What does my grief teach me?

-3- A message of support from my ancestors.

-4- How do I open myself to self-compassion?

Journal Prompts

Choose one or more of these questions each week to reflect and explore here or in your journal.

What is my relationship to grief? What thoughts, feelings, and sensations arise when I reflect on my grief?

What am I currently grieving? How do I mourn my losses?

What have I avoided grieving?

What would a compassionate mourning practice look like for me? How can I honor my grief without getting stuck in it?

How do I show myself compassion?

What is it like to witness grief in others? How do I feel this in my body?

What is my relationship to my ancestors? How would I like to be in relationship with them?

What ancestors do I feel most connected to? How are they supporting me?

What ancestors do I want more connection with?

How do I show my ancestors honor, reverence, and gratitude?

Monthly Rituals

Ritual Tea
Lung Support Tea

- 1 part mullein
- ½ part eucalyptus
- ½ part licorice

Combine all herbs in a jar or teapot. Pour boiling water over the herbs and steep for 20 minutes. Strain.

Full Moon Ritual Bath
Create an herb bundle by tying together whole mullein leaves, roses *(thorns removed)*, and rosemary sprigs *(and any other herbs that speak to you)*. Run a warm bath. Add about a cup of Epsom or sea salt. If desired, add a few drops of eucalyptus oil to the running water. As you soak in the bath, take your herb bundle, and use it to brush yourself, soothing the skin, and clearing your grief from the surface. Soak as long as you like, releasing your sadness to the waters for healing.

New Moon Candle Spell
Use a white or purple candle anointed with Triple Rose oil and sprinkle or roll in dried mullein. Light your candle on your Ancestor's altar (see directions Page 194). Ask for your ancestor's assistance to help you move through grief, enhance your compassion, and receive their support and wisdom as you learn and grow in this life. Take a few deep breaths as you do this.

Practice: Create an Ancestor Altar

All Saint's Day, on November 1st is traditionally a time to honor our ancestors. The first week of November, create an altar with pictures of those who have passed to the next realm: grandparents, parents, aunts, uncles, anyone who is part of your lineage and you feel connected to. If you don't have many photos, place objects that represent them like statues, crystals, candles, or antiques. Write their names on cards and place them on the altar to remind you to honor them daily. Place symbolic food or drink items, like dried corn (or any type of food they liked to eat), a small chalice of wine, and/or a few pieces of candy to welcome your ancestors into your home space. Once your altar is complete, light a purple or white candle, cast a sacred circle, and say the following:

"I call on the assistance and guidance of my ancestors who support me on my highest path. I offer gratitude for your wisdom and invite you into my space to help me find clarity, inner peace, and a deeper understanding of who I am and where I come from. Blessed Be."

For the remainder of the month, make a commitment to connect to the Divine and your ancestors every day. As the weather turns cold and the days grow darker, it is a perfect time to be in the energy of stillness and receptivity. Worry less about making plans, manifesting, and acting, and focus more on creating space to receive guidance on the next indicated step, then following through on whatever that is.

A note on benevolent ancestors

Some of our ancestors carry baggage and trauma from this life into the Spirit realms with them. There can be valuable work done with these ancestors. However, it is not our responsibility to heal them—they must choose to heal themselves. Our personal healing work has a positive impact on their healing, which can be a wonderful and powerful experience for all. When asking for assistance from your ancestors in your spellwork and on your spiritual path, I recommend using the following phrases:

"Ancestors who are supporting me for my highest path."
"Benevolent and loving ancestors."
"Well ancestors."

These phrases make it clear to Spirit who you want to assist you in your magic. Ancestors who are clear and supportive of your intentions can ensure that your magic is not influenced by the agendas of ancestors who may have their interests above yours.

Practice: Create a Smoke Blend

Smoke is a beautiful way to honor our ancestors as it travels up to the heavens. It also soothes the lungs (depending on what herbs you include) and cleanses and moves the breath, helping us process and release grief and sadness.

Smoking/incense blends

These blends can be either smoked or burned as incense. Dry them on a baking sheet after harvesting. When they are completely dry, grind them with a mortar and pestle. Recommended herbs:

- Mullein (as your base, use 2 parts of this and one part of everything else)
- Lemon Balm
- Motherwort
- Lavender
- Rose petals

For smoking, you may want to add a bit of water so the herbs aren't too dry when you smoke them. Sometimes I'll store this smoke blend with a fresh orange peel to help keep it from drying out. Roll the herbs in rolling paper, set your intentions, and say a prayer of honoring to your ancestors before smoking.

As incense, light a charcoal round and wait until it's completely lit (it will turn white). Then place one pinch of your mixture at a time on top of the charcoal, wafting the smoke around you, and bringing it into the lungs.

Herbal lung steam, an alternative to smoke medicine is using steam. Boil a few cups of water and transfer to a heat-proof bowl. Add crushed dried mullein leaves, and other herbal allies that resonate for you: rosemary, roses, chamomile, and juniper berries are nice options. Put a towel over your head and your head over the steam. Breathe in the steam for about 10 minutes.

Prepare for the Next Celebration!

Winter Solstice, or Yule, falls on December 21st or 22nd in the Northern Hemisphere and June 21st and 22nd in the Southern Hemisphere. It is a time of darkness, and also a welcoming of the light as the nights begin to shorten.

Items to prepare, gather, and/or place on your altar:

Holly, pine, and evergreens to decorate your home

Incense and bells for cleansing and brightening the energy of your home

White, green, red, and gold candles

Pears, oranges, cranberries, cookies, and sweets

Yeasted fruit breads, such as German Stollen, Mexican Three Kings Bread, and Italian Panettone

Ginger, peppermint, nutmeg, bay leaves, cinnamon, and cloves

Frankincense and myrrh resin to burn or essential oils to diffuse

Depiction of Mother Mary, angels, or other deities you associate with this time of year

Monthly Reflections

What was most challenging for me this month?

What was most rewarding? What growth have I witnessed in myself?

Magical associations to the Grieving Woman:

Tree, herb, flower, and plant allies I worked with:

Animal allies I worked with:

Stone allies I worked with:

Songs:

Scents:

Food and drink:

People, Deities, Role Models:

My Personal Practices: *What am I learning about my personal magic through these practices?*

Permission

What is…is that I'm sad as hell, and it's blindsided me. What is…is that I'm scared and feel very alone. What is…is that I'm not holding it together very well. What is…is that my panic response has been activated and it's on its own program now.

What is…is that I know my own resiliency. What is…is that I trust the wheel of time, the turning of the Earth, and changing of the seasons. What feels like a shitshow is really parts of my life rearranging themselves to be more in alignment with my heart and soul. And I have feelings about that.

What is…is grief.
My baby getting older.
My body feeling tired.
Old dreams dying to make space for the new ones.
My inner little girl who is terrified of what she might become and how she might screw up, feeling abandoned, and lonely, and overwhelmed.

I sit in the muck of these pieces of life rearranging themselves. I sink deeper.
Deeper.
I sink past the old muscle memory of resistance, judgment, and fear.
Down I go,
down to the heavy sensation of acceptance.

Here I am in the muck. I am becoming the muck, muscles turning into thick mush, my bones feeling soft and wobbly, and my heart dissolving into cool, damp, gooey release.

I give myself permission to sink here—to rest in grief and loneliness and the fear of the unknown.

Below the whispers of "keep it together" lies the truth.

"You have permission to be a shitshow."

Shit grows the most beautiful gardens.

Chapter Twelve
DECEMBER

"I am the Crone. I peer between the worlds."

DECEMBER BRINGS the Winter Solstice, the longest nights of the year, and marks endings and beginnings. During this time of year, our culture encourages a ramping up of activities (think parties, shopping, gift wrapping, and all the busyness). On the other hand, our bodies ask for deep rest and restoration. This month is an invitation to trust ourselves and our needs, to honor our bodies' cycles, and stop pleasing everyone else while we burn ourselves out!

Wisdom ✦ Rest ✦ Hope ✦ Dreaming

The Crone

The Crone is the elder; the Wise Woman who invites us to sit at her feet and hear her stories and lessons. She is powerfully psychic and sees in the dark places, deeply attuned to her dreams and visions as they are inspired by Spirit. Nearing the end of her physical life, the Crone has little to lose and cares not about impressing people. She honors herself and the Divine above all.

The Wound: Burnout

The Healing: Rest

Element: Water/Earth

Plant Ally: Mugwort
Mugwort is deceptively common but holds incredible magical powers. This plant ally is highly protective and supportive of feminine energy and magic. It is also used to inspire dreams and visions, opening gateways for our psychic powers.

Animal Ally: Owl
Owls are nocturnal and have heightened senses in the dark. They are bringers of wisdom and are powerful hunters and seers. The spirit of the owl helps with vision and trusting the deep wisdom of the Crone within you.

Stone Ally: Moonstone
This crystal helps us tune into the energy of the moon, the Divine Feminine, and our inner wisdom. It is both soft and powerful, magical in its ability to tune into the power of quiet, rest, and silence so we can receive guidance from the Divine.

Monthly Themes

Wisdom embodies crone energy. When we deeply engage in our healing work, learning the lessons of our life experiences, growing and transforming, honoring the role of Spirit, and surrendering on our journeys, we begin to access true wisdom. We understand with humility that the wisdom we bring to the world is ours alone, not to be imposed on others, but willingly and lovingly shared where it is useful. Wisdom teaches us there is always more to learn, grow, and be transformed. We are a work in progress. We are at peace where we are now, knowing the world keeps turning, and we keep changing.

Rest is required for healing, restoration, and growth. Inner knowing comes through inner stillness. Rest is the antidote to our cultural programming, the value that being busy means we are valuable. The more exhausted we are, the harder we work to prove ourselves worthy in the world. It is time to challenge this programming. Rest is the answer. Our bodies are designed to heal naturally, but only if rest is available to replenish and nourish all systems of the body.

Dreams. When we rest deeply and are comfortable with stillness, our dreams communicate with us. Visions, spiritual guidance, inner knowing, and brilliant ideas come through the dream space, a space that must be cultivated and tended to, outside of the busy thinking mind. The dark days of winter are the time of rest and dreaming, inspiring us with new vision for the next growth cycle.

Hope comes from dreams. Even in the darkest times, we know the light will return. Through our visions, we see what is possible. We are creating a new world together with brilliant hope that what we create is something wonderful, greater than any limiting ideas our brains have to offer. During the solstice, we hold the light within us, this light is the hope of the coming Spring, new birth, and what is being woven by the desires of our hearts, as embodiments of Earth and Spirit.

Affirmations

I am wise and trust my path.

I allow myself to rest.

I hear the messages of my dreams.

Hope is my light in the darkness.

My personal affirmations:

_____

_____

_____

_____

Daily Invocation

I call on my inner Crone to guide me with wisdom and vision. Today, I allow for deep rest when my body asks for it. I listen to the messages of my dreams and honor the dark time as a needed respite from action, and allow for new desires and visions to come through me. Today, I honor hope as a beacon through the darkness of winter. Blessed Be.

My personal intentions and prayers:

_____

_____

_____

_____

_____

_____

_____

_____

Journey with your Crone Meditation

Find a comfortable place to sit or lie where you will not be disturbed. Drop into the breath, scanning the body from head-to-toe. Notice all the sensations that arise in your body as you breathe, without agenda or judgment. Now, imagine walking along a path, the path is your journey through this life. Imagine your experiences and memories as a landscape. Notice what it looks like. Look to the path behind you (your past). Do you see mountains you've climbed, forests you've navigated, rivers you've splashed through? What does the journey of your life look and feel like? Notice the path you are standing on at this moment. Explore the path in detail. Notice how you feel at this point in your journey. Now look at the path ahead of you (your future). Notice what the path looks like. Farther along this path, you see an old woman carrying a candle, lighting your way. She is your inner Crone. See her—how does she look at you? What is she beckoning you toward? What is she showing you on your path? How do you feel when you see her? As you begin to walk toward her, she walks toward you, too. When you meet, greet her, and allow her to greet you as she wishes. Is she warm and loving? Is she fierce and wizened? What does your inner Crone want to tell you? She leans and whispers something in your ear, wisdom to help you on your journey ahead. Receive the message and bring it into your heart. Offer her gratitude for lighting your way. As your crone continues on the path, know that she is always standing before you, offering wisdom, light, and guidance with each step you take. When you feel ready, leave this place and return your awareness to your body and the room around you. Open your eyes and come back to the present moment.

Reflections on this meditation:

CARD SPREAD

-1-
Guidance on making space for rest during this time.

-2-
A message of support from my Inner Crone.

-3-
What is Spirit dreaming for me?

-4-
How do I open myself to vision from Spirit?

Journal Prompts

Choose one or more of these questions each week to reflect and explore here or in your journal.

What is my relationship to my inner Crone? How do I envision her? What does she feel/think/believe?

What crones do I admire and receive support from, both in the physical and spiritual realms?

What is my relationship to rest? Do I create space for rest in my life? What would be needed to allow me more space for rest?

What doubts or fears do I hold about the future?

Where do I feel weary? How do I nurture myself when I feel overwhelmed, burnt out, and exhausted?

How do I perceive my future self?

What is my vision for the future? What are my dreams? What gives me hope?

What themes are most prevalent in my dreams?

What do these themes represent in my waking life?

What is my relationship to the unknown, mystical, and inexplicable?

Monthly Rituals

Ritual Tea
Dream Tea

- 1 part passionflower
- 1 part skullcap
- 1 part mugwort
- 1 part damiana
- ½ part rose petal
- ¼ part dried rosemary

Combine all herbs in a jar or teapot. Pour boiling water over herbs and steep for 20 minutes. Strain. Add any kind of milk you like.

Full Moon Ritual Bath
Create a salt blend of Epsom or sea salt, mugwort, chamomile flowers, and frankincense and balsam fir essential oils (or other pine essential oil). As you run the warm bath, add the herbs and a cup of milk. Light some incense, and place a few candles around your bath. Create a beautiful ceremonial space for this ritual bath. As you soak, read this month's meditation to yourself or listen to a recording of it, and call on your Inner Crone. See your third-eye opening and activating. Allow yourself to receive wisdom or messages. Dream into your hopes and intentions for the winter months and the next growth cycle.

New Moon Candle Spell
Use a white or purple candle, anoint with Triple Rose oil (see Page 44) and sprinkle or roll in mugwort and pine needles. As you light your candle, ask for wisdom and clarity of vision. During this time of rest, ask for messages from Spirit to visit your dreams and guidance for how to tend to yourself. Bring Divine light into your body and allow it to light up and warm your cells, blood, bones, and organs. Offer thanks to your ancestors, inner Crone, and Higher Self.

Practice: Dream Work

Dream work is highly personal and unique to everyone because your subconscious mind gives you a story with symbols to decipher. Often, the meaning isn't clear right away. But the more we work with our dreams, the better we get at understanding what they mean. Working with dreams is a doorway to understanding the spirit realms at work in our physical experience.

Keep a journal by your bed and when you wake up each morning, write anything and everything you remember about your dreams. If you can't remember your dreams, write about how you feel upon waking, what emotions, thoughts, sensations are you having. The threshold between sleep and waking is a potent time of magic, and a place we receive wisdom and messages from Spirit. Pay attention to these thresholds and open yourself to the messages and visions that come during this time.

As you keep your dream journal, notice if there are recurring themes. One recurring theme in my dreams is my vision being blurred, which tells me I am missing something, not seeing something clearly. This helps me understand when I need to seek and cultivate clarity, or when I need to trust and surrender to Spirit. Allow your intuition to guide you in making sense of the imagery and experiences of your dreams. Use your subconscious to open associations with symbols and dream images.

Before falling asleep, ask Spirit or your Higher Self for messages in your dreams. Sometimes we don't need to know what they mean or what is being communicated—just having the dream is enough.

Practice: Make a Dream Pouch

To help you connect with your dreams, visions, and messages from Spirit, make a Dream Pouch. This can go under your pillow at night, or carried with you during ceremony, ritual, and anytime you are practicing divination or want to be connected to your deep wisdom.

In a small canvas or muslin bag, place the following:
- Mugwort – for protection, dreams, and divination
- Juniper needles/berries – for ancestral support and protection, connection to spirit
- Lavender flowers – for balance, calming, and vision
- Sage – purity, grounding, wisdom
- Yarrow – protection and boundaries, psychic abilities, strength, and confidence
- Labradorite – for dreams and wisdom
- Moonstone – for seeing your path clearly and manifesting intentions
- Rose petals or a few drops of your Triple Rose oil – Divine love, connection, and protection

Just a pinch of each of these will be enough. You can also add charms or decoration to the outside to enhance your intentions. Cleanse your pouch with sacred smoke and charge it under the full moon, calling on your inner Crone and Spirit to imbue it with powers to dream, see in the darkness, and access your inner wisdom. Offer thanks.

Celebrate Winter Solstice!

December 21st and 22nd in the Northern Hemisphere
June 21st and 22nd in the Southern Hemisphere

The Winter Solstice, also called Yule, is the longest night of the year. It marks the dying of the sun and its rebirth the following morning. It is a time of deep rest and release, embracing death and darkness, and holding onto the hope of the coming spring. Yule celebrations commonly entail calling light into the home, holding light within ourselves to guide us through the dark months and dreaming our desires for the coming of spring.

During this season, I honor Mother Mary as a guide and support. She endured such challenge and hardship to give birth to the "light of the world." She is an unconditional, loving presence, helpful in healing and bringer of miracles. In some Christian traditions, she is the embodiment of the Divine Feminine, referred to as the Mother of God and Queen of Heaven. To honor Mary during this time, offer gold or white candles, roses (or other flowers), prayer beads, and incense on your altar.

Winter is the time of honoring the element of Earth, deep wisdom, stillness, and dreams in the darkness. Here are some ideas to work with the element of Earth and the season of winter.

Season: Winter

Element: Earth

Tarot: Suit of Pentacles

Direction: North

Time of day: Midnight

Symbology: Death, darkness, rest, and wisdom

Body: Bones

Magical tools: stones and crystals, salt, dirt, wood, and bone

We are of the Earth, so as we honor and connect with our bodies, we honor and connect with her. She speaks to us through our bodies, the root of our physical nature. We work with Earth magic when we need security, in abundance/prosperity spells, when we are working with birth and growth and Mothering energy. What is your relationship to the Earth? Do you talk to her? Try it sometime. Go for a hike among the trees and see what they have to say to you. How do you treat your physical body and your surroundings? These are all part of Earth energy. See what it feels like to greet Mother Earth every morning and love on your body as an extension of her.

Ways to connect to Earth Magic
- take off your shoes and walk barefoot on the Earth. Dig your hands into the dirt and feel her gentle rotation under your feet. Ground yourself by meditating and sending roots down to the Earth. Listen to rocks and crystals (sustainably mined, always).
- Salt magic: Salt is a simple form of Earth magic. As a crystal, it holds intention. We can speak intentions into the salt we use in our food, and make ritual salts to protect a ceremonial circle, our home and physical spaces, and anoint candles for other spell work. You can add herbs, oils, and flowers to salt to make a ritual salt bath.
- You can keep a bowl of salt on a windowsill or altar to absorb negative energy and cleanse the energy of a space (make sure to change it from time-to-time).

Yule logs

To make a Yule log to honor the dying sun and keep light in your home, take a piece of firewood and decorate it with greenery like cedar, fir, holly, rosemary, juniper, or rowan. Fasten the greenery with twine.

On the Solstice, burn your yule log, sending blessings into the fire for the year ahead. Offer thanks for the year that has passed and bring the light of the fire into your heart, asking to carry the light within you through the dark months of winter. You can also burn your Spirit Box that you made in January, surrendering all your struggles to the Divine.

Raunaechte

In Germany it is an old tradition to honor the 12 days of Christmas as Raunaechte, a time of quiet, darkness, and banishing demons. For twelve days, from December 21st to January 1st, burn incense or herbs every day in your home. Light candles to banish the darkness and welcome the light. Take time to dream and journal about what this time of year means to you and the medicine you receive from it.

Monthly Reflections

What was most challenging for me this month?

_____
_____
_____

What was most rewarding? What growth have I witnessed in myself?

_____
_____
_____

Magical associations to the Crone:

_____
_____
_____

Tree, herb, flower, and plant allies I worked with:

_____
_____
_____

Animal allies I worked with:

_____
_____
_____

Stone allies I worked with:

Songs:

Scents:

Food and drink:

People, Deities, Role Models:

Personal Practices: *What am I learning about my personal magic through these practices?*

Dream into Being

We are the dreamers
We are the visionaries
We are the boat rockers
The wave makers
The justice seekers

We are the healers
The wise ones
The teachers
Our medicine comes through our words
Our hands
Our songs
Our love for the Earth and all beings

We are remembering our power
Breathing into it
Expanding into it
Learning to stand in it
without fear
Or apology

We are dreaming the world into being
Weaving our dreams into the fabric of a new world
We are creating
building
shaping
conjuring
connecting
calling it forth
in beauty
in gratitude
in collaboration and inspiration

Our ancestors are here
The grandmothers at our backs

Guiding our steps,
Reminding us of who we really are
Of whom they had forgotten they were, too.

We are traveling.

We are crossing these lands,
Crossing oceans and continents
To return to our sacred places
They carry the secrets of our past

We gather our skirts,
toes digging into the Earth
with each step we take
Moving with purpose
We know where we are going

We are remembering.

We are dreaming the new world into being.

NOW WHAT?

BY THE END of this year, you will have the basic tools, practices, and supplies you need to bring magic into your life every day and embody your powers of intuition, manifestation, and connection to the Divine. Hopefully, you have a clear idea of what approaches work best for you and which do not. Take this knowledge and wisdom with you to apply in the coming years, honing your magical and spiritual practices and increase their potency and efficacy.

I encourage you to take some time to reflect on the growth, learning, and realizations that happened this year. Allow it to inform your desires and intentions for next year. Do some journaling about the portal between the changing of the year, and how you experience the energy of this time. Some questions to consider:

What was most impactful for me this year?

What lessons do I want to take with me into next year?

How would I like to deepen in my spiritual work and grow personally next year?

What was most challenging for me?

What do I still need to release?

What have I learned about who I am becoming?

What magic worked for me and what didn't?

It is also important to think about how our magic and spiritual work impact our communities and the world that is emerging in these times. Now that you understand yourself, your desires, your shadows, and your spiritual helpers, what role do you wish to play in creating the world that is unfolding? Manifestation magic is not only personal, it is inherently communal. Everything we do has a ripple effect. Our outer worlds are a reflection of our inner worlds; are you cultivating generosity, love, equality, and justice within yourself? How can you take this into your external world, holding systems and leaders accountable for the perpetuation of old, unloving ways of being?

I hope your magical practices clarify your personal intentions for the changes you wish to see in the world, both inside of you and outside of you. You are a being of infinite power, with assistance from the Spiritual realms you create a life and a world filled with beauty, ease, and abundance. Trust this and move forward in joy and gratitude for this sacred life we have been given. Blessed be.

RESOURCES

This is a list of my personal library and resources that have guided my own journey and influenced my personal practices. It is by no means a comprehensive list! Consider this a starting point to other resources—there is so much valuable information out there. Please do your own research and find the teachers, books, and courses that align for you.

Narrative, storytelling, and mythology:

The writings and teachings of Dr. Sharon Blackie, especially *If Women Rose Rooted*

The writings and teachings of Dr. Clarissa Pinkola Estes, especially *Women Who Run with the Wolves*

Spirituality, magic, and witchcraft

Books:

Animal Speak by Ted Andrews

Cottage Witchery: Natural Magick for Hearth and Home by Ellen Dugan

Jambalaya: the Natural Woman's Book by Luisah Teish

Llewellyn's Sabbats Almanac (Llewellyn's is a well-known publisher of resources of magic; they have books on tarot, astrology, magickal correspondences, daily spells, and much more to explore and learn from)

Many Moons Workbooks and Planners by Sarah Faith Gottesdiener

The Mist-Filled Path by Frank MacEowen

Mother Rising by Yana Cortlund, Barb Lucke, and Donna Miller Watelet

The Modern Witchcraft Guide to the Wheel of the Year by Judy Ann Nock

Paths to Recovery: Al Anon's Steps, Traditions and Concepts

Prayers of Honoring, Boundaries and Protection, and *Goldmining the Shadows* by Pixie Lighthorse

The Spiral Dance by Starhawk

Tarot Basics by Evelin Burger and Johannes Fiebig

To Ride a Silver Broomstick by Silver RavenWolf

A Woman's Way through the Twelve Steps by Stephanie S. Covington

Landscape of Mothers by Jill Doneen

Tarot and Oracle decks:

    Goddess Power Oracle Deck and Guidebook by Colette Baron Reid

    Sacred Rebels Oracle by Alana Fairchild and Autumn Skye Morrison

    Shining Woman Tarot Deck by Rachel Pollack

    Smith-Waite Tarot Deck, Centennial Edition

    The Weavers' Oracle: Journey Cards and Travel Guide by Carolyn Hillyer

    The Wild Unknown Animal Spirit Deck by Kim Krans

Modern witches/teachers I follow (not listed elsewhere):

    Temperance Alden

    Milla Prince

    J. Allen Cross

    Juliet Diaz

    Lindsay Mack

    Lizzy Jeff

Anti-racism and de-colonizing Educators and Authors:

    Michelle Cassandra Johnson, author of *Skill in Action and Finding Refuge*

    Resmaa Menakem, author of *My Grandmother's Hands*

    Dr. Rocio Rosales Mesa at https://www.drrosalesmeza.com/

    Layla F. Saad, author of *Me and White Supremacy*

    Myisha T. Hill, creator of Check your Privilege at https://checkyourprivilege.co/

ACKNOWLEDGMENT

Writing this book has been both a beautiful gift and immense challenge for me, which I find that most things that are truly worth doing tend to be. I could not have done it without the support of my family, community, and my spiritual path.

I'd first like to thank my editor, designer, and book witch, Heather Dakota. Thank you for walking me through this process with patience, wisdom, and vision, as I stumbled through my creative process not knowing where we'd end up. I'm proud of the book we created together.

To my husband Joe; thank you for standing by my side, for believing in my dreams and supporting me as I tirelessly pursue them. Thank you for trusting me enough to take big leaps of faith with me in my work and in our family, and thanks for being yourself—a brilliant, loving, creative, optimistic, hardworking, gentle and supportive human in the world. You have shown me true commitment and fidelity and I'm so happy we picked each other to create a life together.

To my first born, Joseph Augustus; you were the inspiration to me to stop playing my life small and be true to my heart's path. Thank you for the push I needed to become the mother and role-model I wanted to be for you, to show you that all things are possible, that you are capable of doing great things, that you are a magical creature who deserves to live a life that is aligned with your values, beliefs, and desires.

And to my second child, still growing and preparing to come into this world, thank you for coming when you did, for giving me the creative fire to write this book at the same time as creating you, for making me a mother for a second time. It is a spiritual path I would never have guessed would bring me so much deep joy and satisfaction.

I want to acknowledge the cities of Glastonbury and Edinburgh, where the seeds of this book were planted. The magic and awakenings that happened for me there are still within my cells. They will always be a place of power and inspiration to me.

ABOUT THE AUTHOR

Sharon J. Balsamo is a writer, witch, therapist, coach, mama, and dreamer of dreams. She holds a Master of Science in Clinical Mental Health Counseling and is a Licensed Professional Counselor working in private practice in Central Oregon. She identifies as a queer woman, a settler of European descent (German, Celtic and Italian) living on the occupied lands of the Wasco, Warm Springs, and Pauite tribes, and uses the pronouns she/her. A world traveler and spiritual seeker, Sharon has training in Brainspotting, Huna, Holotropic Breathwork, Psychodrama, Dialectical Behavioral Therapy, Interpersonal Neurobiology, Focusing and Hakomi somatic therapies, and has gone on spiritual pilgrimages to the Big Island of Hawaii, Bali, Glastonbury, Edinburgh, Guatemala, and more (she's particularly a fan of volcanoes, if you can't tell). Originally raised in Virginia, Sharon now lives outside of Bend, Oregon with her magical family.

Learn more about the author and her offerings at **www.thewakingjourney.com**. She currently sees individual clients in her private practice in Central Oregon, offers women's groups, workshops, and breathwork experiences in her community, and occasionally facilitates transformational retreats, incorporating the teachings, practices, and principles in this book. Sign up for her newsletter through the website to stay updated on upcoming events and to receive random magical nuggets of wisdom as they come.

Titles for Meditations

Jan: Ground and Connect Meditation

Feb: Cord Cutting and Cleansing Meditation

Mar: Safe Space Meditation

Apr: Worshipping the Maiden Meditation

May: Inner Teacher Meditation

June: Expansion Meditation

July: Energy Hygiene and Protection Meditation

Aug: Snake Meditation

Sept: Tending to the Womb-space Meditation

Oct: Inner Wise Woman Meditation

Nov: Welcoming the Ancestors Meditation

Dec: Journey with your Crone Meditation

www.ingramcontent.com/pod-product-compliance
Lightning Source LLC
Chambersburg PA
CBHW081305070526
44578CB00006B/811